"This highly accessible, engaging and timely book explores the recent history of homicide investigation in England and Wales, drawing primarily upon the perspectives of those involved in these investigations, past and present. The book fills an important gap in knowledge about the causes and consequences of change in homicide investigation."

Fiona Brookman, *Professor of Criminology,*
University of South Wales

A Recent History of Homicide Investigation

Drawing on in-depth research, including interviews with former and serving detectives, this book explores how homicide investigation in England and Wales has changed since the 1980s and the opportunities and challenges that have arisen as a consequence. The investigation of homicide in England and Wales became subject to significant reform in the 1980s, when the inquiry into the Yorkshire Ripper investigation identified numerous failings in how the hunt for Peter Sutcliffe was conducted. These investigations have been subject to criticism and change from that moment onwards. This book explores how change has shaped every facet of these investigations, with four main areas identified: science and technology; legislation, regulation and guidance; investigative practice; and lastly, detective status and culture. The work shows that change has been the result of four primary catalysts: a growing preoccupation with risk, the changing political landscape, reactions to miscarriages of justice and other cases, and advances in science and technology. What has been lost and gained as a result of change is also explored. It has, in many ways, been positive as scientific and technological advances allow investigators to plot an offender's movements and draw a clearer picture of what transpired. However, change has created today's more risk-averse homicide detectives, who must manage the vast amounts of technological information that modern-day investigations now generate. They must also contend with a raft of legislation and guidance that now govern investigations and budget pressures not faced by their predecessors. The book will be a valuable resource for students, researchers and policymakers in the areas of criminal law and procedure, criminal justice, criminology, and policing.

Sophie Pike is Senior Lecturer in Criminology, Bath Spa University, UK.

Routledge Contemporary Issues in Criminal Justice and Procedure

Series Editor Ed Johnston
is a Senior Lecturer in Law, Bristol Law School, University of the West of England (UWE), UK.

See more at www.routledge.com/Routledge-Research-in-Legal-History/book-series/CONTEMPCJP

A Recent History of Homicide Investigation

Changes and Implications for Criminal Justice in England and Wales

Sophie Pike

LONDON AND NEW YORK

First published 2023
by Routledge
4 Park Square, Milton Park, Abingdon, Oxon OX14 4RN

and by Routledge
605 Third Avenue, New York, NY 10158

Routledge is an imprint of the Taylor & Francis Group, an informa business

© 2023 Sophie Pike

British Library Cataloguing-in-Publication Data
A catalogue record for this book is available from the British Library

Library of Congress Cataloging-in-Publication Data
Names: Pike, Sophie, author.
Title: A recent history of homicide investigation : changes and implications for criminal justice in England and Wales / Sophie Pike.
Description: Abingdon, Oxon ; New York, NY : Routledge, 2023. | Series: Routledge contemporary issues in criminal justice and procedure | Includes bibliographical references and index.
Identifiers: LCCN 2022028690 | ISBN 9781032062341 (hardback) | ISBN 9781032062365 (paperback) | ISBN 9781003201298 (ebook)
Subjects: LCSH: Police—Great Britain. | Homicide investigation—Great Britain. | Criminal investigation—Great Britain.
Classification: LCC HV8196.A3 P55 2023 | DDC 363.20941—dc23/eng/20220815
LC record available at https://lccn.loc.gov/2022028690

ISBN: 978-1-032-06234-1 (hbk)
ISBN: 978-1-032-06236-5 (pbk)
ISBN: 978-1-003-20129-8 (ebk)

DOI: 10.4324/9781003201298

Typeset in Times New Roman
by Apex CoVantage, LLC

Contents

Introduction
The Need to Pursue All Lines of Enquiry

On Friday 2 January 1981 Peter Sutcliffe, a lorry driver from Yorkshire in England, was arrested for the murders of 13 women and the attacks of seven others (Byford, 1981). The apprehension of the man, labelled the "Yorkshire Ripper", signalled the end of a six-year investigation by West Yorkshire Police but marked the beginning of significant change within the police as this was an investigation that was engulfed by criticism. In the decades that have followed, however, the investigation of homicide in England and Wales has continued to find itself at the centre of controversy as other cases have emerged highlighting flaws within the investigative process. In response, there have been calls of "This must not happen again" and changes made, including increased legislation and oversight of detective work. This has taken place against a backdrop of rapidly evolving and ever more complex scientific and technological techniques.

Despite such turbulence surrounding homicide investigation, it has been largely exempt from academic scrutiny. Some 40 years after the enquiry into the crimes of Peter Sutcliffe, the following are questions that now demand attention: In what ways has the investigation of homicide changed? What other factors have driven change? What is the impact of these changes? It is the aim of this book to address these and, in doing so, provide a detailed account of the recent history of homicide investigation in England and Wales.

The Sutcliffe case was clearly an important moment in the history of major crime investigation and provides a starting point for our examination of the investigation of homicide. A brief review of the history of investigative work, however, reveals a chequered past, and it is a consideration of this that begins our exploration.

The Emergence of Criminal Investigation

The police service was established in 1829 (Emsley, 2008), and its initial focus was on crime prevention and order maintenance, as opposed to

DOI: 10.4324/9781003201298-1

investigation and detection (Matassa and Newburn, 2007). In 1842, how-ever, the Metropolitan Police (MET) were forced to introduce individuals whose role it was to investigate crime as they had started to receive "unfa-vourable" attention from the media, leading commissioners to recommend the creation of a small detective branch (Morris, 2007, p. 17). Despite this, controversy continued. The investigation into the Road Hill House murders in 1860 was one such example, with the detective leading the investiga-tion, Jonathan Whicher, deemed incompetent in his handling of the case (Morris, 2007). This might explain why the detective department continued to be slow in its development, with the number of officers standing at just 15, some 25 years after its introduction (Shpayer-Makov, 2004). As Rubin (2011, p. 417) explains, "For much of the nineteenth century detective work had been the Cinderella of the police service", with minimal collaboration between police services across the country.

The Metropolitan Police established a Criminal Investigation Depart-ment (CID) in the late 1870s (Maguire, 2008), which replaced the detec-tive branch. It was an attempt to develop uniformity in the investigative work that was becoming a part of the police role (Shpayer-Makov, 2004). This was also a response to concerns that had by this time arisen about the supervision of detectives as corruption was becoming apparent, with three chief inspectors at one time being arrested for such offences (Rubin, 2011). The introduction of the CID, however, did little to assuage concerns, and it was labelled a "firm within the firm" (Morris, 2007, p. 21). Furthermore, it was only the MET that housed a permanent CID (Innes, 2002), and so other forces had to call upon a detective from Scotland Yard for assistance when investigating serious crimes (Mooney, 2010). There were also concerns at this time around the lack of detective training, and a 1919 review of police training in England and Wales "recommended against specialist training for detectives" (Morris, 2007, p. 24). The role was seen to be akin to a craft, and the skills were varied and dependent on individuals and the location of the police force (Stelfox, 2009).

The Hunt for the "Yorkshire Ripper", the Byford Enquiry and Continuing Concern

The investigation into the crimes of Peter Sutcliffe was unprecedented in terms of the rarity of such offending and the public fear it engendered and its scale. The police were faced with a huge volume of information to navigate, as evidenced by the efforts to identify tyre tracks left at one crime scene, which resulted in a list of 53,000 registered vehicle owners (Byford, 1981). This was also an investigation that was beset by criticism, and the Byford enquiry that was established to review it identified significant failings that prompted reforms that were to significantly mould the investigation of major crime (Brain, 2010; Byford, 1981). This was the first time that a homicide investigation had become subject to considerable scrutiny and reform, but it would not be the last. High-profile miscarriages of justice and criticism of other investigations continued to arise. The murder of Stephen Lawrence in 1993 would exemplify this.

Sir William Macpherson, who led the enquiry into the MET's handling of this investigation, found that it was "marred by a combination of professional incompetence, institutional racism and a failure of leadership" (Macpherson, 1999, p. 317). This "raised once again the vexed issues of police racism and discrimination" (Bowling, Reiner and Sheptycki, 2019, p. 90), but what also became clear was that many of the concerns that surrounded this investigation had been seen before during the Byford enquiry some two decades previously (Innes, 2002). This leads us to begin to question the efficacy of the changes that emerged as a result of that earlier enquiry.

Furthermore, in a review of enquiries into major crime investigations, Roycroft (2008) identifies themes, ranging from leadership to information management, that were apparent across many different cases that have been investigated over the years. To illustrate, a lack of leadership was identified during the Byford and Macpherson enquiries but also during those that followed the 2002 murders of Holly Wells and Jessica Chapman and the crimes of Harold Shipman (Roycroft, 2008). Problems with information management were also identified in the case of Holly Wells and Jessica Chapman, where the Home Office Large Major Enquiry System (HOLMES), established in the aftermath of the Byford enquiry, struggled to "cope with the volume of information" (Roycroft, 2008, p. 52). Additionally, the enquiry into the investigation of the murder of Damilola Taylor in 2000 found that not all lines of enquiry were fully pursued (Roycroft, 2008).

Homicide Investigation Under the Microscope?

Homicide attracts significant academic, media and public interest (Brookman, Maguire and Maguire, 2017), and much of the media interest "misrepresents its extent and nature" (Pike, Allsop and Brookman, 2020, p. 19). Stelfox (2015) suggests that the public hold high expectations about the way in which the police deal with these crimes, but as we saw in the previous section, these expectations are not always met.

Despite this, homicide investigation and detective work remain relatively neglected by the academic literature (Brookman and Innes, 2013; Stelfox, 2015), and much of the empirical research that has been conducted originates from the United States (Brookman, 2015) rather than England and Wales.

The work that has emanated out of England and Wales has often focused on particular aspects of homicide investigation. Allsop (2018) examined police cold case investigations, Brookman and Innes (2013) explored what constitutes success and Hobbs (1988) looked at detective culture. Some works have aimed to explore change. Stelfox (2015) wrote about the development of homicide investigation to identify where savings might be made in light of funding cuts. In his book exploring why changes in policing have taken place, Savage (2008) suggested that failings in major crime investigations have been responsible for driving change.

This book, by comparison, will take a holistic approach in presenting a qualitative exploration of the recent history of homicide investigation in England and Wales, one that begins when it was firmly placed under the spotlight and continues into the late 2010s. Evidence of the necessity for such attention is apparent. In addition to certain cases illustrating that major crime investigation remains imperfect, the police service has experienced substantial budget cuts (Her Majesty's Inspectorate of Constabulary [HMIC], 2014), and challenges with detective recruitment have also been identified (HMIC, 2017). In the few years since this research was conducted, these issues show no signs of abating as a campaign that was initiated in 2020 by the Police Federation (no date) titled "Detectives in Crisis" highlights the challenges that continue to be faced in relation to detective recruitment. More broadly, at the time of writing, the MET specifically finds itself at the centre of criticism with the police commissioner Dame Cressida Dick resigning following a series of damaging controversies. These included a report by the Independent Office for Police Conduct (IOPC, 2022) identifying significant failings in conduct at one police station, including sexual harassment and the deletion of material that was relevant to a criminal investigation. This followed the 2021 conviction of two MET police officers for taking photographs of murder victims Bibaa Henry and Nicole Smallman at a crime scene and sharing the images with other officers using WhatsApp (*BBC*, 2021a). Lastly, and moving beyond the MET, the homicide detection rate has seen a slight decline from around 94% in the 1960s to around 90% since 2000 (Brookman, Maguire and Maguire, 2018), which although still high is perhaps surprising given the tools that are now available to investigators. Homicide investigation is undoubtedly in need of closer attention.

The Research

This book presents the key findings that emerged from qualitative doctoral research that was completed in 2018 (Pike, 2018) and provides perspectives that are rarely drawn on – the perspectives of those who have been involved in the investigation of homicide, past and present. These were primarily gathered through semi-structured interviews that I conducted with 27 former and serving homicide detectives. Both male and female detectives were interviewed, which also served to provide me with some understanding of the challenges faced by female detectives working in a historically male dominated world. The twenty-seven participants consisted of 14 former and 13 serving detectives and represented various ranks, including detective chief inspectors (DCIs) and former detectives who were now working as major crime review officers. Those interviewed also had experience in different aspects of homicide investigation, including those who had worked as part of outside enquiry teams (OETs) and as family liaison officers (FLOs). The sample included former detectives whose careers had begun in the late 1960s and a serving detective who had recently acted as senior investigating officer (SIO) for the first time, enhancing that "past and present" perspective that was necessary to obtain the required data. Throughout the book SD and FD are adopted to denote when the data have been collected from a serving (SD) or former (FD) detective, although readers should be aware that many of the former detectives that were interviewed were still working for the police service in other capacities. This is acknowledged where relevant.

The case files of three homicides were also analysed; a homicide from the 1980s that was unsolved at the time of the research, a still-unsolved homicide from the 1990s and a homicide from the 2000s that had been solved. Although these were obtained from one police force, the diverse and unusual nature of the cases served to counter concerns around representation. I also spent two days with the Major Crime Investigation Team (MCIT) of one force, during which time I attended briefings and two days observing SIO training organised by another force. Seven police forces were represented (four in England and three in Wales) through the interviews, case file analysis, and observations. These included smaller police forces covering rural areas and larger city-based police forces.

The data from this research have informed two journal articles to date (Allsop and Pike, 2019; Brookman, Pike and Maguire, 2019). Although some similar arguments are raised both in this book and in those articles, the context of the discussions differs, and other data in addition to mine are drawn on. Specifically, the focus of these papers, in particular, was first on the different ways in which detectives in the US and the UK have responded to legal reform (Brookman, Pike and Maguire, 2019) and second on the impact of changes to investigations on cold cases (Allsop and Pike, 2019). Reference to these discussions is made where relevant.

It is important to note at this juncture that the term "homicide" encompasses many different types of killings, from a case in which a man kills his former partner to killings that take place as a result of rivalry between gangs. It is diverse and complex, and a whole host of explanations have been offered to try and understand its occurrence (Pike, Allsop and Brookman, 2020). This book, however, is concerned with exploring the overarching changes that will have impacted upon the investigation of all homicides in some way. Support for this approach is evident in the existence of legislation and guidance that has been introduced over the years to regulate homicide investigation, irrespective of the circumstances. The guidance contained in the Murder Investigation Manual, or MIM, for example, did not differentiate between different types of homicide (Association of Chief Police Officers, 2006).

I cannot, of course, claim that the findings that emerged from this research, and which are to be set out in this book, can be applied universally or that all detectives will have the same view. Similarly, it is acknowledged that not all of the changes that will have taken place over the years are mentioned in this book and that there may be other cases that are considered to have been influential in some way that are not discussed here. This is a consequence of several factors, including space constraints as well as, more importantly, the data that were gathered and the specific experiences of those spoken to for the research. Nevertheless, it has been suggested that homicide investigation is underexplored, at least in part, because of the challenges associated with gaining access to this "closed world" (Brookman, 2015, p. 236), and so, whilst some caution is urged, it remains the case that the research that underpins this book will provide the reader with a detailed insight into the recent history of these investigations and the challenges that may lie ahead.

The Layout of the Book

Chapter one will show that the investigation of homicide in England and Wales has been subject to extensive change since the 1980s and that this has been the result of numerous societal and organisational influences. In Chapter two our focus shifts to a consideration of the many opportunities that change has presented, which will include those that extensive scientific and technological developments have offered. What we will also see here, however, is that new opportunities have brought new challenges, which will also be contemplated. In Chapter three we consider those more overarching issues that today's detectives are now facing. These include an apparent increase in risk aversion and the impact of budget cuts. The final chapter offers a consideration of the implications of the issues discussed throughout the book as we draw together the past, present and future of homicide investigation in England and Wales.

Conclusion

In this introduction I have sought to briefly outline the emergence of criminal investigation in England and Wales and what we know about just some of the challenges that it has faced. It has been shown that homicide investigation has been subject to much controversy and change since its inception and that this continues. It has, however, remained relatively free of academic attention, and so contrary to what is required of today's homicide detectives, not all lines of enquiry have been explored. In the chapter that follows, we begin to address this as we seek to identify the ways in which homicide investigations have changed and the driving forces behind these.

1 "I Don't Think It's Been a Revolution, It's Been an Evolution"

Exploring How and Why Homicide Investigations Have Changed

The first response that may come to mind as we consider the question "How have homicide investigations changed?" is scientific and technological advances, or more specifically deoxyribonucleic acid, better known as DNA, because of its prevalence in media representations that so often see it play a central role in the successful solving of crime (Durnal, 2010). In the first half of this chapter, however, it will be shown that change has been far more pervasive than this, with virtually no aspect of these investigations escaping reform. A consideration of *why* these changes have taken place follows. In the introduction to this book the role of high-profile cases in driving change was referenced, but again, we will see that the picture is more complicated. What we will see is that change has seemingly been the result of several different driving forces.

In What Ways Have Homicide Investigations Changed?

When I began to interview the homicide detectives that participated in the research, the first question that I wanted to ask was whether they could identify a significant change that occurred in respect of homicide investigations and which took place during their career. I had, perhaps naively, anticipated that they would be able to single out one key development, but this proved not to be the case:

> I joined February 4th 1980 . . . I left August of 2011 . . . it's changed beyond all recognition.
>
> (FD 12)

The responses to this question revealed that change has been extensive, and consequently numerous answers were given by each respondent. Despite this, it was possible to identify four main areas of change under which various developments could be situated. Each of these are now discussed in

DOI: 10.4324/9781003201298-2

turn, beginning perhaps where we might expect, with scientific and technological developments.

Science and Technology

Developments in science and technology over the past 40 years and beyond
have been extensive, and much of the world has been transformed with the
emergence of the internet, mobile phones and the growth in social media.
To illustrate, a report from Ofcom (2020) reveals that in the UK alone 80%
of adults now own a smartphone and 72% of adults have a social media
profile. Policing does not exist "in a social, political or economic vacuum"
(Rogers and Gravelle, 2012, p. 420), and so it has not been immune from
these wider societal developments. Therefore, although changes across the
entire process of homicide investigation were identified, those in respect of
science and technology were unanimously considered by the detectives to
have been the most significant. When we consider the relatively basic tools
that detectives had to rely on historically, it is understandable that changes
in this area seemed to prominently come to mind when they were asked this
first question:

> Today the police have the ability to pick up the microscopic little bits
> we would never have even considered to be evidence back in 1975/1976
> that's now key to an investigation.
>
> (FD 5)

The specific changes cited were the following:

- deoxyribonucleic acid (DNA).
- Home Office Large Major Enquiry System (HOLMES).
- mobile phones.
- closed-circuit television (CCTV).
- social media.

Recognition of the fact that science and technology has greatly influenced
homicide investigation has been documented elsewhere. Innes (2010,
p. 33) points out that the role of the homicide detective is "increasingly
shaped by the use of scientific methods and technologies", and it is also
reflected in the growing importance of the "science" arm of the "art, craft
and science" model of detective work (Westera et al., 2016). Originating
from Reppetto's (1978) research on detective work in the US and explored
subsequently by Innes (2010) and Tong and Bowling (2006, p. 323), this
model has been defined as a "framework for examining what detectives

do and the challenging nature of their work". Whilst the "science" element refers to the use of scientific and technological techniques, the "art" and "craft" refers to the innovative approaches adopted by detectives when faced with a particularly complex investigation (Innes, 2010). Specifically, the "art" element refers to the "assumption that individuals have innate qualities to perform their role . . . qualities [that] cannot be taught" (O'Neill, 2018, p. 28). Meanwhile, "craft" is "dominated by the idea that experience and time spent as an investigator is superior to book learning and science" (O'Neill, 2018, p. 31). This model will be referred to and discussed further in Chapter two. The importance of scientific and technological tools is not unique to homicide investigation, and they have become an important part of policing in general. The extent of developments in terms of policing more broadly is summarised by Bowling, Reiner and Sheptycki (2019, p. 220):

> The contemporary police officer's primary visual engagement with the external environment is mediated by a squad car's windscreen and the on-board computer screen. Even the foot or bicycle patrol officer – a chief symbolic representation of the community policing ideal – is primarily attuned to the two-way radio, smartphone, and other systems and process and serve up formal police knowledge of "the community".

What will become clear in the chapters that follow is that developments in this area have, yes, presented opportunities but also new challenges. Given the growth of the scientific and technological capabilities, it is perhaps unsurprising that a growth in legislation, regulation and guidance has also taken place and was also considered by the participants to be important.

Legislation, Regulation and Guidance

The Judges' Rules, which provided guidance for the police during investigations, have previously been described as vague and difficult to enforce (Maguire, 1988), and in the 1980s they were replaced by the Police and Criminal Evidence Act (PACE) 1984. PACE was, according to Cape and Young (2008, p. 1), an "innovative and controversial attempt to regulate the investigation of crime and, in particular, the detention and questioning of suspects". As a headline at the time revealed this was the "biggest change for 50 years" in respect of policing (Gibb, 1985). This legislation has clearly become an integral part of criminal investigations:

> PACE. That's it. Completely changed the way we operate.

(FD 2)

The changes that it led to were significant, for they saw the introduction of Codes of Practice that offered "detailed procedures regulating stop and search; search and seizure, arrest; detention and questioning of suspects; identification parades; tape and video recording and dealing with terror suspects" (Bowling, Reiner and Sheptycki, 2019, p. 238). PACE was not the only piece of legislation that has emerged and was considered a significant development. The respondents also cited the introduction of the Criminal Procedures and Investigations Act (CPIA) 1996, which regulates criminal investigations and prosecutions and sets out that investigators must "maintain records of the investigation, pursue all reasonable lines of enquiry, disclose the material that they uncover to all parties in the trial" (Stelfox, 2009, p. 67). The Murder Investigation Manual (MIM) was also reported to be an important development. This was designed to provide something of a blueprint for investigators investigating cases of homicide and came soon after the enquiry into the death of Stephen Lawrence (O'Neill, 2018), with further editions following. In a sign of the continued evolution of policing, in 2021 the National Police Chiefs' Council (NPCC) published a new version of the MIM titled the Major Crime Investigation Manual (MCIM), which incorporates guidance for homicide and other major crimes investigations. The 2006 MIM that was in circulation at the time that I conducted the research was described by one participant as

the Senior Investigating Officer's (SIOs) bible, a very, very good book. (FD 4)

Also mentioned, although with less regularity, was the introduction of the Human Rights Act (HRA) 1998 and the Regulation of Investigatory Powers Act (RIPA) 2000, with the impact described as follows:

RIPA has had the biggest impact because before we would follow people around and we would do it without any documentation, whereas now if you're running an operation and you're doing anything whereby you might be intruding on an individual's private life, or in anyway keeping them under review for any period of time, then you technically need that in place. (FD 9)

Importantly, what became apparent during these discussions was that detectives have apparently become more and more risk averse, and this was linked to a perceived rise in burdensome bureaucracy. This will be discussed in Chapter three. What is also noteworthy at this point is the role that particular cases have played in driving legislative change. The wrongful conviction of three youths was pivotal in paving the way for PACE. The CPIA was introduced as a result of miscarriage of justice. This was caused by a failure to disclose material that could have aided the defence in the case of Stefan Kiszko (Stelfox, 2009) and following the recommendations of the Royal Commission on Criminal Justice (Hannibal and Mountford, 2002). We will return to such matters in the latter part of this chapter.

Investigative Practice

Perhaps unsurprisingly given the developments that have been discussed so far, changes in respect of the day-to-day running of investigations were said to have been substantial. In what at this point seems to resemble a "domino effect", changes in one area of investigations appear to then have an effect on another. Changes to the day-to-day running of investigations became apparent as it was described how the police now retain a core team, and so the way in which teams are drawn together is no longer ad hoc, as was explained by one former detective:

> There was no bespoke investigation squad, it was all a question of who was on duty at the time and who can come across to work on it.
>
> (FD 1)

The establishment of teams *dedicated* to the investigation of major crime was also described as being significant as, unlike those with just a core team, police services with dedicated teams no longer have to draft in additional officers and often now also feature civilian investigators. Homicide investigation teams today were described as being like "well-oiled machines" (SD 8).

Policing has faced substantial spending cuts as "expenditure by police forces has been cut in real terms by 18% between 2010–11 and 2015–16 with the component of police spending centrally funded by the Home Office falling by an even larger amount" (Crawford, Disney and Innes, 2015, p. 2). This helps us to understand why the way in which investigations are resourced is another area that was reported to have changed. Those who worked on homicide investigations during the 1970s and 1980s described how money was "thrown at" an investigation but explained how budgets today are now a key priority for SIOs.

There was further development related to the interview process. Numerous detectives reported that with the introduction of models of interviewing, this has become more professional and structured than it was historically when obtaining a confession was considered to be the goal of the interview. This was also linked to the introduction of PACE, which began to regulate the ways in which police interviews were conducted and was a response to cases in which issues with interviews were found to have been linked to miscarriages of justice:

> I would say that the interview of a suspect has moved away from the goal of securing a confession which is what it always was when they oppressed and they poorly treated in order to gain a confession, that was the goal of an interview years ago . . . Quite often now the role of an interview is to block off defences.
>
> (SD 11)

Investigative practice has developed in other respects. As a consequence of investigations becoming more complex, driven at least in part by scientific and technological developments, SIOs must delegate more work to members of the team and draw on outside expertise. Additionally, learning post-investigation has also become an important aspect of homicide investigations today with references made to domestic homicide reviews (DHRs) and a more general sense of a willingness to reflect upon investigations and a move away from a "well, what do you know better than me?" (FD 9) mindset.

Finally, and as further evidence of a "domino effect" of change, the participants repeatedly explained that the volume of work that must be conducted is far greater than had been experienced in previous years. This, along with the other changes discussed so far, might be said to have culminated in the final area of change that we will now consider, those in respect of detective status and culture.

Detective Status and Culture

Detective culture has not received much attention within the academic literature; certainly "cop culture" has been subject to closer examination (Reiner, 2010). Of course, this might be explained by the fact that homicide investigation, which is one area in which detectives operate, has been described as a "closed world" (Brookman, 2015, p. 236). This does not, however, reduce the necessity of considering developments in this area, and it did become apparent that this is yet another area that seemingly no longer resembles the past.

To illustrate, many detectives that I spoke to explained that the kudos that was once associated with being a detective has lessened, and the drinking and "longest hours" culture once synonymous with detective work, and which was documented by Hobbs (1988), has largely disappeared. Additionally the mindset of investigators and their approach to investigations was said to have altered. Their approach historically was said to have been characterised by tunnel vision and a "We need to get our man" attitude, whereas the detectives reported to me that they are now more open-minded:

> Going back further to the start of my career the pressure was purely on catching the person . . . from what I saw then . . . It was almost that egotistical approach . . . "have you got him yet? Have you got him in custody? Is he in?' These were always the questions. "Who is it? Why are you so slow?" It's all about the ego of the SIO to get that person in custody. But for me there's a sea change now . . . I think the focus now is "are you doing it right? Are you protecting us from risk?"
>
> (SD 8)

The relatively scant work to have examined detective culture has found that detectives were more likely to "sail close to the wind" when it came to rule breaking, which was linked to the work being less visible than that of uniformed officers (Maguire and Norris, 1992, p. 21). The findings of this research would suggest that this is no longer the case. There are, however, indications that detective culture has perhaps not evolved quite as much as this overview might suggest. As was alluded to in the introduction, more recent concerns regarding the conduct of the police also casts some doubt on the extent to which they can be said to now be fully open-minded when conducting homicide investigations. It is relevant to note here, as it might offer an insight into why mindsets have reportedly changed, that the detectives also spoke of the changes that have taken place in respect of training. The introduction of the Professionalising Investigation Programme (PIP) in 2005 was an attempt to standardise training as previously "informal apprenticeship was the rule" (Morris, 2007, p. 17) and "learning on the job" the primary way in which detectives learnt (Maguire and Norris, 1992, p. 22).

It is clear that there is not an aspect of homicide investigation that has escaped some form of adjustment across this time period, and it seems that change in one area of homicide investigations triggers change in another. However, a closer examination of what *drives* change reveals a more complex process that appears less linear than a "domino effect" analogy might suggest. Although it is possible to isolate four pivotal driving forces of change, it will become evident in the next section that there is considerable overlap amongst these and that there exist other elements at play that have a role in creating the conditions for change to occur. Ultimately, when it comes to *explaining* change, it might be necessary to alter our analogies as it seems it might be understood less as a "domino effect" and more as a "perfect storm".

Why Have Homicide Investigations Changed?

The detectives' explanations for change often referred to the capitalisation of developments in science and technology, reactions to certain cases and the general recognition that detective work was in need of reform. These explanations will, at least to some extent, reflect the personal experiences of those that I spoke to and be influenced by the time periods during which they worked, the cases that they dealt with, their personal views and other factors. The literature around policing and criminal investigation echoes their position but also reveals other explanations (see, for example, Stelfox, 2009). By drawing on what the research uncovered and what the literature reveals, it is possible to deduce that change has been the result of four key triggers:

- a preoccupation with risk.
- the changing political landscape.
- reactions to miscarriages of justice and investigative errors.
- advances in science and technology.

A Preoccupation With Risk

There has been a growing preoccupation with risk in late modern society, leading to efforts to manage it (Kemshall, 2003). Homicide investigation is no exception, and a preoccupation with risk appears to have played an important role in driving change. In particular, it is an aversion to risk that can be said to have driven many of the changes that homicide investigations have experienced. Moreover, it is the status that homicide has that helps us to understand why this has had such an impact. High-profile homicide cases, which Innes (2001, para 2.7) refers to as "signal crimes", "become the focus for a concentrated version of otherwise more nebulous popular fears and concerns. Such crimes symbolically display the nature of a problem and establish a need in the popular psyche for something to be done". This is linked to the concern that society has with managing risk, and according to Innes (2001, para 2.4), the measures of control that result from demands for "something to be done" gradually expand in response to new problems in what he calls "control creep"[1]. As was established in the introduction to this book during the discussion about the crimes of Peter Sutcliffe, change has sometimes taken place in response to cases in which

---

1 Innes (2001, notes) explains that "control creep" is derived from "surveillance creep", introduced by Marx (1988).

errors have been made in a bid to prevent the same mistakes from being repeated. This has prompted efforts to formalise and regulate homicide investigation, as is evident in the introduction of legislation designed to govern the practices of detectives and the professionalisation of interviewing and detective training.

Aversion to risk might also be deemed responsible for the increased volume of work that must now be conducted, which participants partly attributed to risk aversion on the part of the police service. Littlechild (2008, p. 665) argues that efforts to determine and minimise risk have led to an "increasing tendency to regulate professionals and their decision-making", and this has undeniably been the case for homicide investigation, as it has in other areas such as social services. In an examination of how to reduce risk in child protection, Munro (2010, p. 1139) explains that "compliance with existing procedures, rules and audit regimes is a key focus of appraisal rather than whether those procedures, rules and so on are the best way of protecting children". Munro (2010) also makes reference to a report by Lord Laming which discussed progress in child protection following the publication of the Laming report of 2003. The Laming report was produced following an enquiry into the murder of eight-year-old Victoria Climbié by her great-aunt and her boyfriend in February 2000, following what the consultant, who treated Victoria before her death, described as "the worst case of child abuse and neglect that I have ever seen" (Laming, 2003, p. 1). In the 2009 report on the progress that has been made since, Laming (2009, p. 33) writes that "professional practice and judgement . . . are being compromised by an over-complicated, lengthy and tick-box assessment and recording system". Although Laming (2009) is referring to the specific methods of recording used by professionals working in child protection, similar concerns have been raised by detectives investigating homicide, as is illustrated here and which will be discussed further in Chapter three:

We had a murder where a guy killed his girlfriend, drove her into the police station, comes in the police station and says "I killed my girlfriend", even that enquiry was seven or eight months, hundreds of statements and actions and you think "well, is that efficient?" and I mean you say there's no price on justice, but I do think well when you look at the public purse and staff resources and shortages, something like that sure should be a case of "right, we're going to focus on this, he's saying he's killed her, there's no-one else involved, he's saying he's had a moment of madness, well the experts can work around that", but no, we still, and a lot of it is SIO driven because they are afraid of that review because there's always someone that knows better, there's always "well, why didn't you do this? Why didn't you do that? Why didn't you get this expert?"

(SD 21)

The focus upon risk and risk management similarly explains why learning from investigations has become increasingly important over the years as the participants reported:

> It's quite interesting that a lot of those things now have moved on, but there's always things that just need to be improved . . . as we learn from every investigation . . . we have tried over the years to . . . learn from those mistakes and to give SIOs of the future the best possible tools to make sure we are not repeating old mistakes.

(FD 9)

Reviews of murder investigations are one arena in which learning now takes place and Jones, Grieve and Milne (2008, p. 477) note that a key question for these is "Could this have been prevented?" That investigators are now concerned with preventing homicides has also been considered a consequence of the emphasis upon risk management and risk minimisation according to Brookman and Innes (2013). Indeed, reducing and preventing homicide has become an important measure of success in investigative work (Brookman and Innes, 2013).

The Changing Political Landscape

"Law and order" did not feature strongly in political debates until the late 1970s, when the conservative government turned its attention to it and increased spending on the police (Downes and Morgan, 2007; Downes and Morgan, 2012). Prior to this time the police had held a "relatively privileged status" (Golding and Savage, 2008, p. 736), and they had been left untouched by many of the reforms that other public services were experiencing under the rise of "new public management" (NPM) (James, 2013). NPM is described by Glynn and Murphy (1996, p. 125) as "characterised by the adoption of quasi-markets and contracting processes and the application of explicit standards and measures of performance". The relationship between police and governments, however, changed during the 1980s and 1990s as effectiveness and efficiency became increasingly important and control centralised. The police were no longer exempt from the public service reform that was materialising as part of the NPM agenda. The emphasis on managerialist principles is something also recognised as being a driver for change in policing more generally (Bryett, 1999; Savage, 2007; van Dijk, Hoogewoning and

Punch, 2015). Although it did not impact upon criminal investigation in the manner that it did uniformed departments, it is suggested that these principles have indirectly impacted on the investigation of homicide (James, 2013). This is recognised by Brookman and Innes (2013), who argue that the emphasis on procedure now evident in homicide investigations can be attributed both to growing concerns with criminal investigations during the 1980s and the drives towards improving efficiency and effectiveness that are linked to NPM.

It is also apparent in the increased numbers of civilian investigators working on homicide investigations. The use of civilians in policing and investigations is not a recent development (Her Majesty's Inspectorate of Constabulary (HMIC), 2004). In the early 1980s civilianisation was considered "a by-word for police economy, efficiency and effectiveness" (HMIC, 2004, p. 39) and was an important part of the value for money agenda (Savage, 2007). However, this might also be explained by the growing complexity of investigations that has followed scientific and technological advances. Civilianisation has grown further since the 2000s with the recognition that more specialist skills are required (Fleming, 2009). This is also further evidence that the view of detective work as sacred or special has diminished (Savage, 2007), which provides us with an explanation for the weakening detective kudos that was discussed earlier.

These explanations also help us to understand why budgets were reported to have become more closely monitored. Broader changes to the economy over the years have meant that police budgets have been cut, leading to spending on the police falling by 20% between 2011 and 2015 (HMIC, 2014). This has, in turn, led to a reduction in the numbers of police officers, with them falling by 14%, or 20,000 officers, between 2009 and 2016 (Disney and Simpson, 2017). A report on police effectiveness recognised that because of cuts, "forces have to make difficult decisions about where best to allocate their resources" (HMIC, 2017, p. 10). The evidence that has emerged in recent years suggests that the picture has not improved. Although the government announced a £1.1 billion increase in funding for 2020 to 2021 (GOV.UK, 2020), it has been argued that this does not cover the cuts that were endured as a consequence of austerity (Police Federation, 2021). As will be shown in Chapter three, homicide investigations were reported to have been impacted by changes to budgets, and the consequences of this will be explored.

Heslop (2011) suggests that the advent of NPM can help to explain the increase in bureaucracy in policing that has been identified. Heslop (2011, p. 318) draws on the work of Ritzer (2004) in arguing that NPM has led to the police becoming "McDonaldised". McDonaldisation is "the process by which the principles of the fast-food restaurants are coming to dominate more and more sectors of American society as well as the rest of the world" (Ritzer, 2015, p. 1). There are four key principles that underpin this theory: efficiency, calculability, predictability and control (Ritzer, 2015, pp. 14–16). Heslop (2011, p. 316) suggests that these can be applied to policing, resulting in "McPolicing". Heslop (2011) does not refer to the investigation of homicide, but there are arguably some parallels when we consider the notion of predictability. Ritzer (2015) explains that predictability refers to the customer receiving the same product at whatever McDonald's restaurant they visit. In the context of policing, Heslop (2011, p. 317) argues that over many years the police have aimed to achieve predictability in their unpredictable world through the standardisation of "procedures, services and administrative techniques". Heslop (2011) suggests that this has led to the police service becoming increasingly bureaucratic and, in a return to an earlier point made in this chapter, risk averse.

This growing importance of police reform on political agendas has been referred to as the politicisation of law and order. Savage (2007, p. 329) writes that this has led to the police to be seen as either "too hot to handle" or "too hot to leave alone" (Savage, 2007). Here Savage (2007, p. 328) explains why the police service might be considered "too hot to handle":

> The police may be courted and pandered by government, and as such allowed a privileged status as a public service; "support" for the police can be paraded as evidence of the determination of government to confront law and order. Even if reform of police is considered necessary, the dangers of reform appearing to be "antipolice", an image easily exploited by the opposition (and indeed by the police themselves) may prove fatal to those beliefs.

By contrast, the politicisation of law and order leaves the police vulnerable to blame and them becoming "too hot to leave alone", leading governments to consider reform (Savage, 2007, p. 32). Savage (2007, p. 329) goes on to suggest that the politicisation of law and order has led to an "insatiable public demand for 'more' law and order". Consequently, the police can no longer be left alone by the government (Savage, 2007). It would appear that there has been a particular shift towards the view that the police, and homicide investigation specifically, are "too hot to leave alone" since the 1980s. Many changes that have been implemented have been a consequence of errors during investigations. Homicide detectives today are acutely aware of the consequences that follow investigative failings, and the public expectations of the police in respect of these investigations is very high (Stelfox,

2015). This was something that the detectives interviewed for this study were also very much aware of:

> It's the seriousness of the offence and the public reaction to the murder, if it's a murder it hits the headlines. [There are] the potential sentences people are facing as a result and rightly so, if I was facing that I would hope that somebody would be looking at the case in detail . . . I don't fight against that . . . the case should be scrutinised . . . a case where you have somebody that's lost a loved one then it should come under scrutiny and it should be a good case.
>
> (SD 15)

Reactions to Miscarriages of Justice and Investigative Errors

The role of miscarriages of justice and other investigations in which errors have come to light, in influencing change is well documented (Savage, 2008; Savage, Grieve and Poyser, 2007; Stelfox, 2009), and organisations other than the police can also be driven to change as a consequence of failings (Sendrea, 2017; Weick and Quinn, 1999). Many of the detectives that I interviewed commonly attributed change to the occurrence of miscarriages of justice and other investigations in which errors had been identified. The two cases that were most often mentioned were the crimes of Peter Sutcliffe and the murder of Stephen Lawrence. Those that were interviewed for the study and mentioned these cases had not themselves worked on these particular cases, but their being referenced so often during the research is perhaps to be expected given the time frames that the study was concerned with. It is also indicative of the significance of these cases and the impact that they had.

The role of cases in prompting change might simply be attributed to the fact that homicide is viewed as one of the most shocking crimes and "consistently elicits stronger condemnation" than other offences (Cooney, 2017, p. 54). Therefore, the very status of homicide increases the likelihood that change will take place, as has been suggested elsewhere in this chapter. It is arguably this status that sets homicide apart from other areas of policing and from other organisations. This links to what Innes (2003b, pp. 52–53) refers to as "signal crimes", mentioned earlier, which are defined as "events that, in addition to affecting the immediate participants (i.e. victims, witnesses, offenders) and those known to them, impact in some way upon a wider audience". This illuminates where the pressure on those involved in the investigation of homicide originates but also helps us to understand how, in cases where errors arise, there are measures taken to "put things right". Mawby (2012) explains that miscarriages of justice are especially damaging to the image of the police and their legitimacy, so efforts to change become an important step in repairing that damage and restoring lost legitimacy. This can also be understood within the context of increasing concern with risk, discussed earlier in this chapter, and these cases also make the police "too hot to be left alone" by the government (Savage, 2007). Failings make them a target for blame and, therefore, a target for change.

Building on this are other factors that strengthen the push for change, which suggests that whilst miscarriages of justice and other cases might act as a catalyst for change, the foundations of change might be said to be falling into place over a period of time because of the influence of other factors. Towards the end of the 1970s, rising crime rates were causing concern about criminal investigations and the criminal justice system as a whole (Brain, 2010). Reiner (1992, p. 763) explains that there was a "veritable haemorrhage of public confidence" in the late 1980s and early 1990s. To further our understanding of this, it is necessary to take into account broader societal shifts. In particular, Bryett (1999) argues that improved education, living standards and access to information means that individuals hold higher expectations of those in authority and are more likely to question them. Additionally, escalating media coverage of crime and the growth in social media throughout the 2000s provides the public with a platform that they can use to publicly voice dissent. Of course media coverage of crime is not a recent development with Reiner (2007, p. 304), noting that "criminal biography and pre-execution confessions" were apparent as far back as the seventeenth century. However, it has continued to grow in popularity thanks in part to new forms of media with the emergence of streaming platforms such as Netflix and the growing popularity of true crime podcasts, creating online forums in which a new generation of "armchair detectives" discuss cases. What is common across different forms of media is an interest in homicide and homicide investigations in particular.

To stay with the media, it can be said that its representations of the detective often portray them in a manner that is representative of the "craft" model of detective work that was described earlier in this chapter. Although such representations endure, miscarriages of justice and other investigations have brought the police under further scrutiny, and the public are now intensely aware of failings since they are constantly under the watchful eye of an "unforgiving media" (Beckley and Birkinshaw, 2009, p. 7). Certainly, this research found that homicide detectives were conscious of the media and the widespread negative coverage that problems with investigations would generate:

I would say 99% of SIOs are terrified of the media . . . I'm more comfortable with it now because I've done it more, but I have been absolutely terrified of the media because you're feeling like it's this huge animal that's going to control you and control the investigation and rip you apart really.

(SD 8)

I mean the media frenzy was, well it was unprecedented as far we were concerned, as a force we'd never seen that before and the sheer aggression of the national media was just, well, it was unbelievable really . . . that type of aggression from the national media was being driven by 24 hour news, which wasn't around before.

(SD 13)

Many of the changes that were discussed during the first half of this chapter, including the increased volume of work that modern-day investigations generate and the more complex nature of them, might also be traced back to particular cases. Responses to miscarriages of justice and other cases in which problems have been identified have undoubtedly been instrumental in the introduction of various pieces of legislation, regulation and guidance. It was the failings in the disclosure of evidence in the Kiszko case that contributed to the implementation of the CPIA (Stelfox, 2009), which sets out how the disclosure of evidence should be managed. In 1975, Stefan Kiszko was wrongly convicted for the murder of 11-year-old Lesley Molseed. This wrongful conviction arose as evidence that the killer's semen sample contained sperm was not disclosed to the defence. Kiszko's sample did not contain sperm, and he could therefore have not left the semen that was retrieved from the crime scene (McCartney and Shorter, 2019). Such cases do not just lead to legislative change as, although much attention was rightly focused upon the police and racism, concerns about the quality of the investigation into the 1993 murder of Stephen Lawrence also led to changes that have shaped the investigative process, including the introduction of the MIM.

Such cases can also be considered responsible for changes to the way in which investigative teams are brought together. Innes (2003a) describes how the autocratic model of investigations featured the SIO at the centre, who would hold all the information about a case with less senior officers having little idea as to the details. Innes (2003a) explains that the risk of "tunnel vision" was substantial and that the first signs of change around the organisation of homicide teams became apparent in the 1980s, when there was a move towards a more bureaucratic system. This was a decade in which a large number of miscarriages of justice came to light, which prompted the increased standardisation of procedures. The importance of standardisation was first highlighted in the Byford Report that followed the investigation into the murders committed by Peter Sutcliffe. Byford (1981,

p. 154) urged the Association of Chief Police Officers (ACPO)[2] to "consider the standardisation of Major Incident Room documents and procedures", which triggered a series of changes in the organisation of investigations and in how teams operated. Relatedly, the "confession culture" (Savage and Milne, 2007, p. 614) approach to interviewing of the past led to oppressive questioning and is recognised as being responsible for several miscarriages of justice. However, at first change in this area was quite slow. PACE was an important step forward in regard to interviewing as it stipulated that interviews should be contemporaneously recorded, but it was some years before there were further efforts to formalise the interview process. The subsequent introduction of the PEACE model of interviewing is an example of attempts to further improve interview practices. The PEACE model and the impact of changes to interview practices will be revisited in Chapter two.

The importance that the detectives reported was now placed upon learning from all investigations, as opposed to solely those where something fundamental has "gone wrong", could also be said to originate from instances in which investigations have failed in some way. The Macpherson Report, for example, recommended that Codes of Practice were devised to direct reviews of investigations. Brookman and Lloyd-Evans (2015) highlighted the importance of learning during their research into structured and hot homicide debriefs, whereby the importance of identifying good practice and areas for improvement from each investigation was evident.

The occurrence of miscarriages of justice or other investigations in which problems have been identified may also help to explain some of the reported changes in the detectives' mindset, changes that were discussed by the interviewees in the context of the shifting culture of detective work. Specifically, as was outlined earlier in this chapter, it was suggested that the approach of "We need to get our man whatever the cost" has shifted to one in which the aim is to achieve the right outcome and conduct an investigation that can withstand scrutiny. Reflecting this, in their research exploring what constitutes a successful homicide investigation, Brookman and Innes (2013, p. 300) found that "maintaining the integrity of the investigation" has become increasingly important. Relatedly, the CPIA stipulates that all lines of enquiry are pursued, suggesting that there is no place legally for "tunnel vision". In addition, the MIM stated that "it is not an admission of personal failure to change investigative direction in the light of new material" (Association of Chief Police Officers, 2006, p. 57), which is illustrative of the importance now placed on investigative directions being based on evidence as opposed to suspects chosen by the SIO.

2 In 2015 ACPO was replaced with the National Police Chiefs Council (NPCC).

Advances in Science and Technology

Both the literature and the participants in this research report that the police, like many other organisations, have capitalised upon scientific and technological advances over the past few decades (Senior, Crowther-Dowey and Long, 2007). Certainly, Stelfox (2009) argues that developments in science and technology act as a driver for change in respect of criminal investigations more broadly. These changes have shaped policing in general, and Sanders and Hannem (2012, pp. 389–390) explain that the impact of information technologies in particular over the last 50 years has allowed the police to adopt a proactive, and not merely reactive, approach. Evidently, changes that occur outside of the world of criminal investigations will filter through, providing investigators with new tools to assist them during the course of an investigation.

Research conducted by Bayerl et al. (2013) suggests that the picture is more complex. Exploring the complexity of organisational change that is driven by technology, they looked at the adoption of social media by police forces across Europe, including the UK, to see what factors at a macro level led to these technologies being adopted or not (Bayerl et al., 2013). They found that the implementation of social media varied across Europe. Police in the UK utilised it to engage with the public on a more regular basis than France and Italy, with officers there deeming its use to be "incongruous" with their role, suggesting that how the police perceive their role may have influenced how changes are received (Bayerl et al., 2013, p. 801). Additionally, the authors suggest that economic challenges in the UK might also explain why they have embraced social media since it offers a cheaper way of communicating with the public and gathering information (Bayerl et al., 2013). They also posited that those forces that adopted social media were demonstrating their willingness to make errors "in the eyes of a critical public" (Bayerl et al., 2013, p. 801). Bayerl et al. (2013) were looking at police officers, but there is some alignment with the findings of the current research as it was reported that police service has become more accountable and open about homicide investigations over the years.

A further explanation for the proliferation of science and technology in homicide investigations is that it is linked to the drive towards professionalisation. The professionalisation of the police is not new (Matassa and Newburn, 2007), but it has gained pace over the years. As James (2013, p. 13) writes, "In the recent history of British policing, a consistent theme has been the effort to professionalise what traditionally was craft". Manning (1977) argues that technology is one of a variety of presentation strategies that the police adopt to appear professional. Taking a different perspective,

Green and Gates (2014, p. 85) suggest that as well as these advances helping investigations to become more professional, technology acts as a *moti-
vator* for professionalisation as it has "increased the level of accountability
of the police, with 'citizen journalists' monitoring police operations and
posting on YouTube to go global in an instant". Moving beyond the UK,
this was exemplified in Melbourne, Australia, following the disappearance
of Jill Meagher in 2012. In the aftermath of her disappearance a 'Help Us
Find Jill Meagher' Facebook page was set up and had 90,000 followers
within four days (Milivojevic and McGovern, 2014)[3]. Technology therefore
also places the police under further scrutiny, which can lead to increased
efforts to present a professional image, something that is heightened when
we again take into account the high expectations that the public have of the
police (Stelfox, 2015). It is evident that detectives are under more scrutiny,
and the prevalence of mobile phones and the public using phones to film
them was one example of this. However, it may be more likely that police
officers' interactions with the public might be filmed given the frontline
nature of their work. The fact that homicide detectives also discussed this
may reflect the intensity of the scrutiny that the police service as a whole
feel that they are under.

This research identified that detective work today is perhaps more a "science" than an "art" or "craft". This was also found to be a consequence of
scientific and technological change. Therefore, advances in this area might
provide yet another explanation for the apparent weakening of the detective
status as it is increasingly necessary for them to draw on outside expertise
and delegate more so than they did in the past:

> There's forums for different, specific areas. I've got an account . . . and
> there are lots of areas where you can get advice and specialists . . .
> the National Crime Agency [NCA] have specialist advisors, regional
> advisors . . . if you need an "ologist in whatever, the most bizarre sub-
> ject you can think of because it's relevant to your case, you'd go to
> the [NCA] and they'd research their databases to see if there's an SIO
> around the country whose come across the same issues and put you in

3 Also of note here is what the authors discuss in relation to newsworthiness. Drawing on
Jewkes' (2011) news values they explain how the case met the values required to escalate
the story up the media's agenda (Milivojevic and McGovern, 2014). Jill Meagher would
also meet the criteria required to be considered an "ideal victim" (Christie, 1986). These
concepts help us to understand how "not all homicides are created equally" and that some
will receive greater media attention than others. This has implications for investigations that
remain so reliant on information from the public.

touch with them. There's lots of resources available for consulting with other SIOs and learning from other's experiences".

(SD 15)

Linked to this, such changes can be considered responsible for the increase in civilian investigators as more specialist skills have been required. This is supported by Tong and Bowling (2006, p. 2), who write that "detective work as a science arguably removed some of the mythical and cultural barriers to learning and practising detective work".

Conclusion

With this book examining homicide investigation from a starting point of the 1980s, it is perhaps to be expected that the "answer" to the question "How has the investigation of homicide changed?" is "A lot". Evidently, they have changed in some way across all aspects of investigations. What is also apparent is that how these changes have occurred can be categorised as something of a "perfect storm" since there are numerous factors that have played a part in paving the way for the many changes that have occurred to date. The question that then presents itself is "What has been the impact of these changes?" How have they been advantageous to homicide detectives and homicide investigations? Although the impact of change has been alluded to in our discussions so far, it is the addressing of these questions that will be the specific focus of the next chapter.

2 "The Possibilities Became Endless Overnight"

Change and New Opportunities

In this chapter it will be shown that the detectives that were interviewed for the research considered modern-day homicide investigations to be, put rather simply, better than they were in the past. The advances that have been made in science and technology were considered responsible for many of these positive developments, and in this chapter I outline the ways in which they were said to have assisted investigators. Other positive consequences of change considered in this chapter include the move away from seeking a confession during suspect interviews and the shifting culture that has seen the apparent diminishment of feared SIOs and tunnel vision. However, we will also see that with new opportunities have come new challenges and that whilst, for example, advances in science and technology have certainly had a positive impact, they have prompted concern that the police are "lagging behind" when it comes to attempts to keep up with evolving techniques.

Scientific and Technological Opportunities

As shown in the previous chapter, when the participants that were interviewed were asked to identify a significant change that had taken place during the course of their career, most referred to some form of scientific and/ or technological development. Their careers had spanned large periods of time, and each had witnessed multiple changes; they cited many of these in response to that question. However, DNA, the HOLMES, mobile phones, CCTV and social media were repeatedly mentioned.

To appreciate what was said about the opportunities that such changes have created, it is important to first look back and reflect on the role that science and technology has played in the investigation of homicide historically. The challenges of measuring the early impact of forensic science in particular has been highlighted, (Cooper and Mason, 2009). Nevertheless, the comments of the detectives do shed some light on the role that such

DOI: 10.4324/9781003201298-3

techniques played. To begin, it is important to acknowledge that there are several scientific and technological tools that have a long history of employment in homicide investigations, perhaps one of the most obvious being fingerprinting, and many of these were discussed:

> Fingerprints were our bread and butter because otherwise what you had to rely on was informants, your people coming forward and making statements and saying they saw Joe Bloggs at a certain point at a certain time and . . . fingerprints helped in those days to put somebody, at least at some stage, at the scene.
>
> (FD 12)

The examination of hair and fibres was another technique that was often used in the past, including during the investigation of other crimes such as burglaries:

> Hair samples to test and it was things like fibres really that were very important at the time . . . In the 90s . . . you used to convict people on fibres, murders, but burglaries we used to always check for fibres at the point of entry, the first thing you'd do, I'd have a phone call from scenes of crime officer . . . phone the office and say "look you're looking at a guy with a red jumper with some really fluffy fibres", so if you had a suspect in mind, you'd arrest him and search the house looking for this red fluffy jumper to get a match to the scene.
>
> (SD 8)

There were also scientific tools that were used before DNA emerged and became a critical part of homicide investigations, but these were somewhat limited in what they could achieve. Blood grouping was used, but this would only reveal a person's blood type and would only minimally narrow the pool of suspects:

> It was like blood samples, blood groupings, so you wouldn't obviously have the DNA match but you'd have . . . say it's A or AAA, you'd say "well I know it's a male with AAA blood group kind of thing", I can't even remember them it was such a long time ago, so we'd work on that and you'd have to try and find . . . if you had a suspect your evidential case would be, you know, hypothetically "well, we've taken his blood and he his a AAA so it could be him" . . . so . . . it was very sort of non scientific really that used to form part of the prosecution cases in the past.
>
> (SD 8)

Even computers that today are found in the majority of homes and work-places were, in the 1980s, relatively new and were met with some initial scepticism:

> Computers were quite novel in the early 80s and whilst they were use-ful I think, we used to have people known as the "memory man" and people could remember things . . . "go and speak to that guy, that guy can . . ." . . . and then computers came in and . . . they seemed to take a lot of feeding to produce very little early doors.

> (FD 1)

It might therefore be said that whilst detectives investigating homicide have through the years had access to scientific and technological tools, they were fairly limited. However, it is important to point out that this did not neces-sarily equate to investigations that were poorly conducted or that they did not achieve results. What is clear is that the advances in science and tech-nology that have taken place over the past four decades and longer have provided the police with new tools that they have been able to take advan-tage of and which have transformed the way in which homicides in England and Wales, and globally, are conducted.

The emergence of DNA in particular was considered to have been a significant development. DNA is the "substance that carries an individ-ual's genetic information" (Fraser and Williams, 2009, p. 628). Whilst James Watson, Francis Crick and Maurice Wilkins were awarded the Nobel Prize for discovering the structure of DNA in the 1950s (Taupin, 2013), Alec Jeffreys established the technique of DNA fingerprinting during the 1980s (Roux and Robertson, 2009). Through his work on genetics, Jeffreys found and was able to prove that there are differ-ences between the blood samples of different persons (Bramley, 2009). The benefits that the ability to create DNA profiles have generated are clear when considering that DNA can be obtained from many different sources and in small quantities. As Williams and Johnson (2007) note, it may be retrieved from blood left at a crime scene, hair that has been shed and saliva and nasal secretions. This was a significant advancement on the techniques that were available to detectives previously when, as discussed above, they were only able to determine blood groups and required a lot of blood in order to do so. This was used for the first time in the 1980s to identify the person who had raped and killed teenagers Lynda Mann and Dawn Ashworth in Leicestershire, England. Despite initially evading capture by asking someone else to provide a DNA sam-ple in his name, Colin Pitchfork was later convicted and sentenced to life in prison[1] (White and Greenwood, 1988). Importantly, DNA fingerprinting had exonerated the person whom the police had initially believed to be responsible for the crime.

The detectives that participated in this research spoke of their reaction to the emergence of DNA profiling and how "the possibilities became endless overnight":

> I remember my Detective Inspector going to a seminar about DNA and he came back in the office and said "this DNA thing" and we were crying laughing because he said "they're telling me that one day you'll be able to touch something and someone will come behind with a swab and will be able to tell you exactly who they are, it's ridiculous!" And then a couple of years later I remember I had my first DNA package with a hit of one in a billion that [this person] committed this burglary from a saliva swab, "it can't be right!" We swabbed say a bottle of milk that the burglar drank from and it's unbelievable to think that . . . it was just incredible . . . that was the change of everything. And . . . forensic examination at scenes changed, we looked for different things then and . . . it just . . . the possibilities became sort of endless overnight.
>
> (SD 8)

The positive impact that advances in science and technology have had on the investigation of homicide were clear. As one detective said, "You can implicate or eliminate people with this new technology" (FD 12). Developments in this area, such as those in relation to mobile phones, have also provided investigators with more lines of enquiry to pursue and allowed them to plot an individual's movements and create a clearer picture of what happened:

> I think everybody leaves a footprint and some of the stuff that we've done with phones in the past, charting where people are to make an arrest has been excellent and some of things we are advanced . . . where overlay of phone work with [Automatic Number Plate Recognition] data really does build up a picture as to who's moving in what vehicle

---

1 Colin Pitchfork was released in 2021 after serving 33 years in prison. Although he was subject to extensive licence conditions, he was recalled to prison after two months for approaching young girls (*BBC*, 2021b). The case has raised concerns about the Parole Board process.

therefore affecting an arrest. So . . . we are continuing to . . . invest in the cyber world data, forensics etcetera.

(SD 16)

This was reiterated by another serving detective:

Mobile phones have assisted us . . . immeasurably I would say . . . simple things like text messages back and for, before an incident or a crime happens and more importantly afterwards, you are able to show who the offender has text and what he or she has said and that's a basic.

(SD 8)

It was also apparent that different forms of technology offer different opportunities for those investigating homicide:

I would say social media is more for intelligence, linking people with people, identifying witnesses, so . . . if I'm talking to somebody and passes some information "yes I saw that as well" type of thing, so do all that open source research, but I'd say social media is more for . . . intelligence whereas phones is evidence.

(SD 8)

Others explained that technological evidence, including covert tools, can provide an effective way in which to gather evidence in cases where individuals may be reluctant to speak to the police, something that was often the case in the police force of this interviewee, who is referring to a gang-related homicide, and in Category A[2] investigations where there are no known suspects:

We had a shooting a couple of weeks ago, know who's done it but can't get the evidence. So it's forensics yes, covert techniques are massive in investigations, certainly here where nobody will speak to you in [names police force], they don't speak to the police, so you have to find other ways, to the technology that offenders use that we can exploit

2 The categorisation of homicides helps "guide the initial allocation of resources" (ACPO, 2006, p. 77). A Category A homicide is one of "grave public concern or where vulnerable members of the public are at risk, where the identity of the offender(s) is not apparent, or the investigation and the securing of evidence requires significant resource allocation" (ACPO, 2006, p. 77).

like telephones, laptops in order to get information to piece together a thread of evidence that will prove the case.

(SD 24)

Developments in this area have also proven beneficial when presenting evidence at court:

> Our reliance on eyewitnesses may have diminished a little bit in cases where we have strong scientific evidence . . . well intended, honest, truthful witnesses can be wrong so reliance on science . . . does away with that to a large degree and there's a massive improvement on . . . 20 witnesses all of whom say, quite, rightly, say slightly different things, give slightly different descriptions, if you've got a fingerprint and blood on the weapon it's not as open to challenge as destroying a witness who may be reluctant, nervous, frightened about giving evidence and the implications of being involved in a serious case.

(SD 15)

There is evidently much evidence to suggest that the advent of science and technology has played a significant role in improving the way in which homicide investigations are now conducted. More generally, it was often said that changes in science and technology have made investigations "quicker and easier". The benefits of developments in this regard are undeniable. As Stelfox (2009, p. 35) writes, they "provide investigators with sources of material that their predecessors could only dream of". In addition, scientific and technological advances have enabled investigators to revisit and resolve unsolved, or cold, homicide cases, as argued by Allsop and Pike (2019). However, what is also clear is that these developments have also created new challenges, and it is to these that I now turn.

Victims of Their Own Success?

Although developments in science and technology have, in many ways, made investigations "quicker and easier", a contradiction became apparent as it was also said to have made investigative work increasingly complex. With advances in science and technology has come a wealth of information and data that must now be examined and managed. This has been referred to by Innes (2003a, p. 246) as "information overload", whereby vast amounts of information must be processed and its validity and relevance determined. Such hurdles have seemingly arisen as a result of CCTV, in particular, because of the volume of data that it produces. This is no doubt a consequence of the number of CCTV cameras in England and Wales, with estimates ranging between four and six million cameras in operation (Surveillance Camera Commissioner, 2017). An insight into the scale of the information and data that can be generated is provided here:

> I mean [names operation], for example, which was the CCTV area that I led on . . . if you laid it all end to end we had 11 years of CCTV material, so you can't view all of that so you have to come up with parameters around what you are and are not going to view.
>
> (SD 13)

This issue was also apparent during a review of a homicide case file from the 1990s, which describes that the CCTV footage that was obtained totals "95 hours and it takes 2 days to view a 4-hour tape" (1990s Homicide Case File). The detectives explained that there are challenges associated both with identifying where relevant cameras are as well as with the setting of appropriate parameters and timescales for what is recovered. These discussions also brought to the fore concerns around resources, echoing the findings of Brookman and Jones (2021), and the importance of having trained staff that are able to retrieve CCTV footage:

> The difficulty we find is the practical knowledge of how to download the product before it's recorded over again, because some systems record every 24 hours so say we have a murder, the victim has been dead for 2 or 3 days, you're up against it straightaway with any CCTV enquiries or opportunities because whatever system's in that vicinity they could already have recorded over the offender running off for instance, so for us the challenge is identifying what sort of system is it on: is it a hard drive? Is it a disc? Or is it a tape? All those type of things and getting the engineers out to download it in those timescales.
>
> (SD 8)

SD 8 also described how their police service does not have designated officers with responsibility for CCTV but have "in-house informal experts" who have worked with CCTV evidence over their careers and have developed their expertise in dealing with the systems and are aware of who they need to contact if difficulties arise. National Policing Improvement Agency[3] (NPIA)

---

3 The NPIA was abolished in 2011. Its functions were distributed to other organisations, including the College of Policing (GOV.UK, 2011).

(2011) guidance highlighted the importance of securing CCTV imagery as soon as possible, and so the concerns of the detectives are reinforced. Additionally, because of the challenges that are associated with the retrieval of CCTV evidence, Gerrard (2007, p. 13) stresses that such a task is "clearly a job for specialist staff that have the right equipment and appropriate level of training", which raises questions as to the efficacy of using "informal experts" for this work.

Indeed, one detective described the introduction of a dedicated CCTV recovery unit within their force and the benefits that this had brought. This has enabled them to keep up with changes in technology. This serving detective also explained how the introduction of a dedicated team helps overcome some of the challenges outlined above:

> It cannot be underestimated how good having a set of trained, dedicated people to look into the evidence retrieval and find innovative ways of trawling, understanding the territory because CCTV is one of your staples when it comes to finding out what's happened. And even if there is an incident and there isn't CCTV sometimes inside, you've still got everything that takes place outside, which helps you build a picture.
>
> (SD 20)

It is important to acknowledge that it is not just homicide investigations that are faced with such challenges in light of evolving scientific and technological techniques. One detective explained how counterterrorism investigations have also been impacted by a growing amount of data that needs to be managed:

> I'll give you an example, and this was a counter terrorist investigation, and when you look at it it generated 3,256 exhibits . . . 1,529 statements, 3,014 actions . . . documents collated during the course of the investigation were over 1,900 and then there were 450 CCTV exhibits, 150 systems reviewed . . . and, this is the bit that staggers me, 18.5 years of footage recovered from all possible sources of where that information could be relevant.
>
> (FD 12)

Turning to another issue, it is apparent that the police now also face the challenge of trying to keep up with ever-evolving scientific and technological developments, and there are concerns that they are "lagging behind":

> When you look at phone work, we've really developed a skill about understanding phone data, which has become very cumbersome in

volume but we are able to deduce what's happened in terms of what has gone on and work the data. But the data it continues to expand at an exponential rate thereby we always feel we are behind the curve in terms of being on top of it.

(SD 16)

Similar sentiments were reiterated by others:

Mobile phones were just phones, where phones are computers now aren't they? They're not phones really. The whole police service has had training, I say the whole service certainly sections of it, the government has ploughed a lot of money into trying to develop the forces knowledge of data communications, because the police have been lagging behind.

(FD 2)

The phrase "lagging behind" was used quite regularly during such discussions, and it was apparent that they felt that the capabilities of the police force were not always on a par with what technology today can do because it develops so quickly. During one briefing it was described how the police were unable to examine the mobile phone of one of the suspects in a homicide. In this case the police were specifically unable to access the Black-Berry messages of the persons involved. The issues that certain handsets can present are reflected in the literature. Al Mutawa, Baggili and Marrington (2012) examined BlackBerrys, iPhones and Android handsets in order to identify whether an individual's social networking activity conducted through their phones was stored and so could be subject to examination. Interestingly, they found that "no traces of social networking activities could be recovered from BlackBerry devices", unlike with the Android and iPhone, both of which stored a significant amount of data "that could be recovered and used by the investigator" (Al Mutawa, Baggili and Marrington, 2012, p. 533). Whilst there was no suggestion that this struggle to keep up with wider changes in science and technology had unduly hampered their investigations to any significant degree, it was an issue that was often raised, indicating that it is still a concern of today's detectives.

The development of DNA testing is another example of this issue and which continues to evolve. According to the data, however, this continued evolution has also proved to be challenging for investigators with similar findings uncovered by Brookman, Maguire and Maguire (2018). During the fieldwork a new technique involving DNA testing had recently emerged, DNA 17, and was discussed. DNA 17 is "more sensitive than previous methods, making it possible to gain DNA profiles from poorer quality DNA samples and on ever smaller amounts" (Allsop, 2018, p. 19). It was suggested that DNA 17, which was introduced in July 2014, might even be too sensitive and therefore increase the risk of contamination. As one detective explained:

> Years ago when we needed buckets of blood to get a profile from it wasn't an issue, now you can get DNA maybe from a fingerprint you have to be really careful, even breathing on an item could introduce foreign DNA, so it comes with issues.
>
> (SD 15)

Although advances have been rapid in the last few decades, England and Wales were amongst the last countries in Europe to benefit from DNA 17. During a presentation observed during my research, it was suggested that that the closure of the Forensic Science Service (FSS) in 2012, which saw a move to a "combination of multiple private and police managed services" (Atkin and Roach, 2015, p. 7), has impeded the ability of England and Wales to be at the forefront of developments in this area. As one scientist remarked, England and Wales have gone from "pioneer to nowhere near" (Fieldwork Notes). A QC described the closure of the FSS as "awful" and the new system as "disjointed". This suggests that changes that are driven at government level can affect the resources that are available to the police, resources which play a major role in the investigation of homicide.

The impact of "lagging behind" is also seemingly compounded by the fact that offenders may now have an awareness of science and technology and act accordingly in the aftermath of a crime in attempts to avoid being apprehended:

> I think as we go on further and further and we go to trial and our tactics come out in trial, for instance cell site analysis on telephones, we use that so much now, it's massive and it can really, really nail people. But nowadays people don't use their telephones or leave them at home, they'll drop phones all the time and people having phones every three days because they're so disposable, SIM cards are so disposable, phones are so disposable, they'll get them every 3 or 4 days, so we can never keep track of them or utilise that, so victims of our own success.
>
> (SD 24)

One of the explanations sometimes offered for an apparent awareness of science and technology amongst offenders is the so-called "CSI effect". The "CSI effect" is defined as "the ascribed influence of fictionalised and/ or 'reality-based' television crime programs upon audience knowledge and expectations of the criminal justice process" (Huey, 2010, p. 49). The research in this area offers conflicting evidence as to whether or not offenders have become so forensically aware that they take the necessary precautions to avoid detection. On the one hand, Cole and Dioso-Villa (2009, p. 1344) explain that it is possible to identify several possible results of the "CSI Effect", including the "police chief's effect". The "police chief's effect" is based on the idea that television programmes such as *CSI: Crime Scene Investigation* have taught offenders how to avoid being caught, such as by wearing gloves and cleaning the crime scene (Cole and Dioso-Villa, 2009, p. 1344). They describe this as potentially detrimental to the detection rate.

On the other hand, in a study of sexual homicides, Beauragard and Martineau (2014, p. 219) suggest that whilst there is an apparent greater knowledge about forensics amongst offenders and society in general, "this has not manifested in more cautious offence behaviours". They found that less than half of the offenders in their study took at least one precaution to avoid detection. Baranowski et al. (2018) also failed to provide evidence that such media representations serve as an educational tool for offenders; their data showed that the offenders considered the best source of information to be acquaintances and friends. Baranowski et al. (2018) also discuss the "tech effect" and suggest that it is this rather than the "CSI effect" that is important. This is the idea that individuals have generally become smarter, which is linked to the fact that science and technology have advanced considerably over the years, and whereas historically not many people had heard of DNA, it is now more common, and offenders at least know not to leave their DNA at a scene. Therefore, it is more that they are able to keep up with technological developments than they are being influenced by television shows.

There is further evidence to suggest that the concerns about "lagging behind" are not unfounded, and Her Majesty's Inspectorate of Constabulary[4] (HMIC) acknowledged this in 2016. They found there to be delays in retrieving and examining data from digital devices (HMIC, 2017). Steps have been taken to improve this, and police forces are looking to ensure that only relevant equipment is retrieved from a crime scene to avoid backlogs (HMIC, 2017). Whilst the report does not mention whether this is the case with homicide investigations specifically, it is indicative of the challenges that are being faced as a consequence of technological advances. The report from the following year suggests that there has been some improvement but that "the performance of a small number of forces remains unacceptably poor" in this area (HMIC, 2018, p. 59). Information management is not a

4 In 2017 HMIC assumed responsibility for fire and rescue services also.

new concern. It was a fundamental issue that was identified in the aftermath of the Yorkshire Ripper investigation. However, it has been identified as a recurrent problem both by this research and various public enquiries (HMIC, 2017, 2018; Roycroft, 2008). This matter becomes increasingly pertinent as techniques continue to develop.

From the development of the HOLMES system, continued progress in DNA testing, the prevalence of CCTV, to the use of mobile phone evidence, the growth in scientific and technological evidence over the last few decades has been vast. Comparisons between the homicide case files that were examined reinforce this. The cases from the 1980s and 1990s referred to limited scientific and technological tools, aside from the use of CCTV in the 1990s, but the case from the late 2000s shows more advanced techniques. Alongside CCTV, the file refers to DNA, mobile phones and computer work. One of the primary benefits that the increased availability of such tools and evidence has brought is the new and numerous lines of enquiry that can now be pursued. However, with new opportunities have come new challenges, and those investigating homicide must now contend with extensive amounts of data and techniques that are rapidly evolving and show no signs of abating. As further evidence of this, Amankwaa and McCartney (2021) highlight the use of genealogy in criminal investigation in the United States that, although presenting numerous ethical concerns, provides another example of the ever-expanding toolkit becoming available to homicide detectives. Most notably these techniques were instrumental in the 2018 arrest of the so-called "Golden State Killer", Joseph DiAngelo, who was responsible for many rapes, murders and burglaries across California during the 1970s and 1980s (Compston and Lowbridge, 2018). Interestingly, however, it has been suggested that homicide detectives in the United States face particular challenges when it comes to "securing DNA analyses for evidence they have collected from crime scenes" (Brookman, Pike and Maguire, 2019, p. 761), providing further evidence that with new opportunities come new challenges and that this is the case beyond England and Wales.

Williams and Weetman (2013) argue that there has been a lack of academic attention paid to the role that science and technology play in investigations, noting that attention tends to centre upon volume crime. However, what we do know indicates disparity on this issue. Roycroft (2008) suggested that forensic material contributed to the solution in 38% of homicide cases, whereas Brown and Keppel (2012) found that whilst this evidence was important, it was of less significance than other factors, such as the victim-offender relationship, to solving the case. Further, Brookman, Maguire and Maguire (2018) found that it is not the mere availability of such evidence that leads to the resolution of a case but whether it is used effectively that is key. What has been shown by my research, similarly to Brookman and Jones (2021), is that such advances play a substantial role in investigations.

Detective Skills: Art, Craft or Science?

> The SIO from day one, clearly, you can look through his decision-making, and clearly always thought that the forensic evidence was going to come in because of the nature of the attack, and it never did, and suddenly finds himself six months down the line thinking "where do I go now?"
>
> (SD 13)

It emerged that the importance placed upon science and technology, and DNA especially, has led some detectives, both former and serving, to wonder whether the advent of science and frequent presence of forensic opportunities could lead to difficulties when those rare cases that do not feature any useful forensic evidence arise. The above remark was demonstrative of this concern. Many explained that the retrieval of DNA evidence at a crime scene today would often ensure a relatively swift resolution of the case. By comparison, years ago detectives would not have such opportunities and would investigate the case using house-to-house, local intelligence and other traditional techniques. Additionally, SD 8 explained that because of DNA evidence SIOs today may not be accustomed to running protracted investigations and so can struggle when cases, which do not feature forensic evidence, arise as these may be lengthy investigations. This might explain why some reported that detectives are not as good at speaking to people now as they were historically. FD 3 agreed that the reliance on science has come at the cost of "old-fashioned detective work" (FD 3) and considered that these skills had been lost "to a certain degree" (FD 3) as a result. It is interesting to note that despite acknowledging that some sort of forensic evidence is usually present, FD 3 discussed a recent case in which there was not any and another recent case in which there was limited forensics. Also referring to this case, SD 13 described this as a situation in which he would like to bring in a team from 20 years ago to see what progress they might make. Although cases such as these are seemingly rare, a second interviewee described an investigation into a homicide that occurred in the late 2000s and that remains unsolved at present, which also features limited forensic evidence despite the brutal nature of the attack as well as a lack of technological evidence such as CCTV.

The belief that the police may be overly reliant on scientific and technological techniques was not held by all, and SD 27 felt strongly that advances in technology and science have not led to the diminishing of detective skills. They argued that the training that is in place and the setup of the Major Incident Room (MIR) would prevent this. SD 27 stated that if this did happen, it would be the result of laziness as opposed to anything else. The detective described DNA evidence as "a bonus" and that a systematic investigation would still be required. Additionally, the concern that detectives rely on scientific and technological evidence is somewhat challenged by the suggestion that such evidence does not play a key role in investigations. Through an examination of homicide case files in Quebec, Brodeur (2009) found that scientific expertise, although important, played a relatively minor role in the majority of cases that were studied. Williams and Johnson (2005) also stress that biological material that may be suitable for DNA testing is rarely recovered from crime scenes, also noting that its role in detections is marginal. The research in relation to the relationship between detective skills and science is similarly conflicting. Exploring the "reliance on science" and detective skills in relation to the investigation of cold cases, Allsop (2018) found that the two worked concurrently with detective skills necessary to ensure the efficient use of science and technology. Conversely, Brookman, Maguire and Maguire (2018) explored what factors lead to homicide cases being solved in the UK and the US. The detectives in their study reported that there was an over-reliance on science and a diminishing of other skills as a result (Brookman, Maguire and Maguire, 2018).

Further, as we mentioned in Chapter one, the literature suggests that detective work has shifted from being an "art" or "craft" to a "science" "as detectives have had to master increasingly complex technology and scientific methods of investigation" (Tong and Bowling, 2006, p. 324), something that the authors recognise as being a change from detective work of the past. The view that detective work now is more of a science was reflected by SD 16:

> I think we went through a phase with detectives where they would like to say it was an "art" whereas the generation that's coming through now would say it was a science and I think there is a bit of an "art" to it so when I'm talking about instinct and listening to that so there will always be an "art" and "science", but I think the balance has shifted for it to be a more systematic, more scientific, more hard data.
>
> (SD 16)

Some of the former detectives highlighted the importance of pursuing all possible lines of enquiry whilst capitalising on the forensic evidence that has been recovered from the scene. They explained that it was important to understand the importance of the forensic evidence but not to be "blinkered" (FD 1) in only pursuing the individual who may have left that evidence behind, for there may be others who were involved in the commission of the offence. They explained that it was a combination of exploring all lines of enquiry whilst making the most of the valuable evidence that you have accumulated.

Whilst advances in technology and science are undeniably significant, one detective emphasised that this information provides only direction, and all possible lines of enquiry must still be explored. This was their response when asked whether science and technology can ever be a hindrance in investigations:

> I think people have got to realise, for example, with intelligence evidence gathered from the mobile phone, it's the phone not the person, that doesn't mean to say that the person's been there, that phone's been there, it's not the person. I think sometimes people can assume the wrong thing by that. ANPR, for example, if that hits somewhere, it's the car, it doesn't tell you who's driving it, but it gives direction . . . were there any pictures taken? Where was it going? Did they call in at the petrol station? Is there footage at the petrol station of the individual? It can give you a new line of inquiry.
>
> (FD 1)

Ultimately, as FD 17, who now works within the police service as a civilian, acknowledged whilst a lack of forensic or technological evidence would be a "knockback" (FD 17) to an investigation, there are so many other lines of enquiry to pursue today that there will always be other avenues to explore, thanks also to these advances. They stressed that investigations should not rely on just one particular line of enquiry. This is especially important when we recall that one of the primary concerns surrounding the use of science and technology in investigations was the difficulties faced in keeping up with developments in this field.

The Professionalisation of Interviews: Slaves to the Model?

As we saw in Chapter one, interviews were considered to be an area that has seen substantial change. When reviewing the comments about the way in which these interviews used to be conducted, it is apparent that reform was considered necessary. Many former detectives told of how prior to the introduction of PACE, suspect interviews were unstructured, not subject to any real scrutiny, and that the focus was very much upon obtaining a confession:

> In the old days you'd always go for a confession if you could.
>
> (FD 10)

The consequences of this were discussed, and it was suggested that it sometimes led to the poor treatment of suspects as they tried to secure that all-important confession:

> I would say that the interview of a suspect has moved away from the goal of securing a confession, which is what it always was when they oppressed and they poorly treated in order to gain a confession that was the goal of an interview years ago.
>
> (SD 15)

As well as the goal being to secure a confession, prior to the establishment of PACE, interviews were not recorded, and instead detectives relied upon their note taking:

> When I first started it was contemporaneous recording, you'd go in, you would interview them and write down afterwards what was said.
>
> (FD 4)

The ramifications of such practices have been well documented elsewhere, and the emphasis that was placed on obtaining a confession has been deemed responsible for several high-profile miscarriages of justice that have occurred. This includes the wrongful conviction of the three youths for the 1972 murder of Maxwell Confait. The conviction had rested on the false confession of one of the youths and which followed oppressive questioning by the police. It was this case that placed attention "firmly on the investigative and specifically the interview process as a major contributor to miscarriages of justice in the UK" (Poyser and Milne, 2011, p. 63). Since then the police interviewing of suspects has "undergone major transformation" (Walsh and Bull, 2010, p. 305), and this was, firstly, down to the introduction of PACE. Secondly, there was the introduction of the PEACE model of interviewing as PACE, according to Walsh and Bull (2010, p. 305), did not on its own lead to "better interviewing methods". PEACE "provides a chronology of events for the interview process" (Cook and Tattersall,

2010, p. 310) and stands for planning and preparation, engage and explain, account, clarify and challenge, closure and evaluation. SD 15 summarised the way in which interviews are now conducted:

> I think we're probably now far more professional in the way that our interviewers are trained; we have different categories of interviewing as somebody progresses in their experience and skill in interviewing. The tier two, tier three, tier five interview advisor levels. So it's probably a much more professionalised and scientific approach to the way in which we interview now.
>
> (SD 15)

Broadly, the interview process today was described as being far more structured than they were previously:

> If you arrest someone it's not a question anymore of "I've dealt with him in the past, I'll give him four or five fags and I'll get him to . . ." They've got to be a lot smarter now and say "right, for everyone that comes in we'll do an interview strategy, we'll know the areas of questioning we want to go into, we'll know when to introduce certain witnesses".
>
> (FD 12)

The introduction of PACE led to the introduction of recording interviews. This has served to lessen the risk of arguments in courts around what was or was not said, arguments that were often the consequence of interviews that were not recorded:

> So you are going from "well I did say, I didn't say, yes you did" to "let's play the tape, here is the audio, here is the video, here's what happened in the interview room" so that's changed out of all recognition.
>
> (FD 4)

Those that discussed the interview agreed that its professionalisation and more structured approach has improved the way in which the interview is conducted:

> I think the professionalisation of it is a good thing overall and I think that the benefits of having a model far outweigh the place we were in before where what made a good interviewer had a bit of mystique around it, so I think that's a good thing.
>
> (SD 15)

On the other hand, it was suggested that one weakness of a more structured approach was that some officers could be fearful of going outside of the model:

> I think the training ought to be geared towards that kind of understanding that the model is just a tool and doesn't need to be followed in such a slavish way, but the interviewer needs to have a clear understanding about what they are trying to achieve from the interview.
>
> (SD 13)

It was suggested that it was both a lack of experience and a fear of getting it wrong that can leave individuals reluctant to step outside the model. This interviewee talks of a fear of getting it wrong and a lack of understanding of the process:

> We have models of interview to follow and I think with less experienced staff they're more reluctant to move away from the model and if all you're doing is being a slave to the model you'll miss some obvious things that are coming up in that interview because you're focused on applying the model and you don't feel confident enough to go outside and just allow the interview to go where the interviewee is taking it . . . it's a fear of getting it wrong and just a lack of understanding really of what the model is actually there for. The model is there to just give you a very basic structure and hopefully make sure you don't miss anything. But, really and truly, interviewers have to be skilled enough to listen to what they're being told and react to that at that time.
>
> (SD 13)

A QC that I interviewed offered a similar viewpoint. He felt that interviewers were nervous of stepping away from the interview plan and suggested that this was a response to past criticism of police interviewing. They went on to describe that because of interview models, the interview has become overly long and complicated and that, by the time the transcripts are prepared for court and "cut down to what is digestible, those subtle points are lost". The advantages of changes to interviewing, however, were acknowledged, and the QC described how whereas in the 1990s much defence work centred upon trying to get interviews excluded because of the way in which they were conducted, this is no longer an issue.

Evidently, the interview has moved from an un-taped, unstructured approach, with the central aim being to achieve a confession, to a far more structured process, a change that is reinforced by the shift in terminology from "interrogation" to "investigative interviewing" (Brookman and Wakefield, 2009). The participants described this as being a largely positive change. Arguably, further evidence of the positive impact of such amendments to interview practices can be found when we consider the approaches adopted in other countries, such as the US, as discussed by Brookman, Pike and Maguire (2019) in a paper that draws on data that feature in this book. Although it is important to be mindful of the shortcomings associated with making comparisons across countries where there are vast differences in respect of how criminal justice systems operate, this does enable us to consider the effectiveness of the changes that have been made in England and Wales. Whereas in England and Wales changes to suspect interviews have come about as a result of the implementation of PACE and PEACE, in the US it was the introduction of the Miranda warnings in 1966 that led to changes in how suspect interviews operated. Echoing the situation in England and Wales in the 1980s were concerns around police interrogation practices in the US for some time before it culminated in the *Miranda v Arizona* ruling. This followed the rape conviction of Ernesto Miranda, a conviction that was largely based on a confession obtained during an interrogation in which Miranda was not informed of his right to a lawyer or of his Fifth Amendment right against self-incrimination (Brookman, Pike and Maguire, 2019). This led to the introduction of the Miranda warnings (or rights as they are also known).

Although their paths to introduction might be similar, there are clear differences with how the Miranda warnings, PACE and PEACE have been responded to by those investigating homicide. Brookman, Pike and Maguire (2019) identified that changes to interviewing practices in England and Wales have been accepted in a way that does not seem to have happened in the US where "learning how to dance around Miranda skilfully seems to be an important rite of passage in the process of becoming a skilled detective" as they employed a number of tactics to circumvent suspects' Miranda rights (Brookman, Pike and Maguire, 2019, p. 43). This does not mean, however, that the approach to interviews in England and Wales is without concern, as we have discussed in this section, where questions were raised about the tendency of some individuals to rigidly follow the interview process.

Life on Mars: The Changing Culture

The majority of the interviewees agreed that detective culture has changed significantly over the years. This was a view held by both the former and serving detectives. The former detectives talked about the culture that used to exist particularly in terms of the working hours and drinking culture. Many remarked that detective work during the 1970s and 1980s was very much like the television series *Life on Mars*, a British show that depicted detective work at this time:

> The most accurate thing I have ever seen is a television series and it's that "Life on Mars". I know its entertainment and all the rest of it, but it was! It was macho, it was very sexist, it was definitely testosterone, it was definitely work hard and play hard, it was all of those things.
>
> (FD 6)

> There's the standing joke amongst detectives: the first time I watched it I thought I was watching a documentary.
>
> (SD 25)

They spoke of a "longest hours" culture and explained that they had to be seen to work the longest hours and be the last to leave whether or not they had work to do. One former detective linked this to the machismo culture that used to surround detectives:

> You've got that whole culture thing then, the hard-nosed, long hours, hard drinking, hard smoking detectives . . . I don't think there is as much machismo, being able to do it, "yeah I've got to work on yet I have done 16 hours, I can do 16 hours and I'm still going out and having 25 beers and then" . . . huge cultural change.
>
> (FD 5)

The detectives' approach to drinking alcohol appeared to be particularly demonstrative of the extent to which the culture has changed. The drinking culture was described as having been an important part of detective work historically (Hobbs, 1988). The importance of the drinking culture was evident in the comments of the detectives who spoke of the social side of attending the ten-week training course. FD 11, for example, described it as "a lot of fun out on the booze every night". FD 12 considered it an integral part of being a detective at this time:

> Young detectives used to save up slush funds to go on those and come back three stone heavier and a few hundred pounds lighter because of the social side of it! All looked upon as an intrinsic part of being a detective.
>
> (FD 12)

SD 8 explained that such importance was placed upon drinking that if you did not engage in it, you were considered odd:

> In years gone by that was the culture, you had to be in the pub afterward or you were seen as odd, you weren't part of the team, it was an equal part of the investigation process really.
>
> (SD 8)

Police services had their own bars that police officers and detectives could drink in. This clearly went some way to facilitating the drinking culture, and many interviewees explained that the closure of these played a part in its decline. However, one serving detective explained how in the early years of her career, detectives would keep alcohol in their desk drawer so that they could have a drink. The following remark demonstrates how the importance of drink was apparent until just ten years ago:

> Years ago there used to be a much more social aspect to being a detective, I mean they had bars in police stations, I mean there were terrible, terrible things that happened like drink driving and bad things, and there were detectives even when I started like 18/19 years ago, it would be after a late you'd go out for a drink, up until probably about 10 years ago that sort of started going. Nowadays it's not a very social environment and I think it stopped when there were no bars in the police stations, which wasn't a wholly bad thing but people then started realising the work life balance.
>
> (SD 24)

When asked what the most important part was of being a detective working on homicide investigations, FD 7 responded that it was bringing some closure for the families as well as the sense of having worked well together as a team, which was "celebrated" in the pub:

> Seeing the bad people locked up and bringing some relief to their families, but there's also a sense within the team as well of a job well done and then you go on the piss.
>
> (FD 7)

It was apparent that the drinking culture historically was significant. However, several detectives commented on the benefits that came with a prevalent drinking culture as some commented that it provided a release after a long and difficult day at work. For some it seemed as though the drinking culture acted almost as a way of providing welfare to the detectives: they could unwind after work and talk about what had happened that day. One former detective described how during the 1980s the welfare was to go down the pub and have a drink and suggested that this was effective. A serving detective who joined the police service in the late 1980s and the CID in 2000 supported this view. He also considered the closure of the police bars to be responsible for the loss of the drinking culture. This participant believed that this proved to be detrimental to the detectives as they lost the opportunity to fully unwind and discuss the case with the rest of the team:

> There is no opportunity now for that generic debrief in an informal setting.
>
> (SD 22)

The drinking culture amongst detectives was therefore seemingly prevalent, but this did serve a purpose in terms of providing a form of welfare to detectives whose work involved long hours and difficult, distressing work. It appears that the loss of that drinking culture may have, in some ways, been detrimental in that they have lost this opportunity to unwind. On the other hand, it should be acknowledged that it is quite possible that the interviewees downplayed the extent of *today's* drinking culture for the purposes of the interview, although the former detectives who remain within the police service did describe its decline. However, it is not just the detectives' drinking habits that have seemingly changed. When discussing culture, the interviewees also spoke about the way in which investigations were approached, which sometimes resulted in a tunnel vision mindset.

The way in which the interviewees described senior detectives and SIOs of the past is indicative of a very different culture of investigative work to what the participants reported exists today:

> It was usually, or historically, a white male old-school detective that's epitomised by your kind of "Ashes to Ashes",[5] you know, "get him, do this, do that".
>
> (SD 20)

---

5 *Ashes to Ashes* was a BBC series and the sequel to *Life on Mars*. Featuring many of the same characters, this series was set in the 1980s.

A similar description was proffered by SD 25, who joined the police service in the mid-1990s:

> They were predominantly men in their late 40s, seasoned detectives and you could see that just by looking at them and they walked around in great suits [laughs] and they weren't quite God status, but they were highly respected individuals.
>
> (SD 25)

SD 8 went further and described SIOs as being feared and that this was the case as late as the early 1990s:

> I think certainly in my career in the early 90s it was all about the SIO, and I say were the men because there weren't any women when I was sort of growing up in the police. SIOs were the Dons, the Gods, the feared ones, were the real tough hard men, egos, very powerful people.
>
> (SD 8)

This status was attributed by some to the years of work that individuals who held these positions had accomplished:

> The Head of CID was probably the most feared man in the force. I remember when I joined as a young PC in uniform, the DI who ran the CID, who ran the detectives, was a feared character, he ran the show really and you wouldn't become a DS or DI without having done years of detective work, which was then deemed to be the hardest work, dealing with the most violent and most dangerous and most risky situations.
>
> (SD 8)

The characteristics of SIOs were also linked to the tendency for investigations to be approached with tunnel vision. Tunnel vision is the focus on one viable suspect or line of enquiry to the exclusion of all others. Rossmo (2016, p. 216) describes the approach, which sees investigators "arresting the first likely suspect, then closing the investigation off to alternative theories, [as] a recipe for disaster". FD 5 gave an example of an SIO who had decided that he was correct about the circumstances of a case:

> He made a decision on a really strange, bizarre, brutal rape. She'd been picked up by a couple, taken to a mountain top, tied up in her car

using seatbelts and raped and dumped her. She was interviewed and she described the car as being a Mitsubishi Colt, a Mitsubishi Stallion so they are quite rare anyway, so he decided she was wrong because she was a "girly" and that in fact it must have been a Datsun Cherry of which there were bloody thousands, so we started working through all the Datsun Cherry's. He also decided that the person that had done it must have come from one of the cities because if he was up here they'd know; they'd have picked him up because the local community would have told us who he was.

(FD 5)

FD 5 went on to explain that the SIO in this case was proved wrong since the offender was found to drive a Colt Stallion and lived in the area. When we consider that SIOs were described as being feared, it is possible to understand why others working with them may have felt unable to question their decision-making, potentially leading to tunnel vision in investigations. Crucially, this mindset is something that has been considered a factor in cases of miscarriages of justice and other flawed investigations. FD 6 described how this might transpire:

I think in a number of miscarriages of justice what can happen is you develop a mind-set where you think for a number of reasons that this person is a suspect, so you stop actually investigating as an investigator and what you do is prove that this suspect committed the murder, which then leads to people trying to do things that actually fit the suspect as opposed to the investigation.

(FD 6)

FD 6 explained that such approaches had taken place within the police service that he had worked:

And I know that happened in [names place] is this idea of "well, you saw who it was they were wearing a hat weren't they? And what colour was the hat?", "I don't know", "It was quite bright wasn't it?", "yeah could've been". And then in an easy . . . you start to develop evidence to fit your suspect.

(FD 6)

FD 6 went on to describe the way in which the SIO motivated the team and the drive towards getting a result:

What used to happen in the 80s, 90s is you'd come in the morning and the DS, the SIO, would motivate you all "you've got to nail this bastard, go and do this, house to house inquiry team I want you to get in the pubs, I want you to get here at 6 o'clock tonight and see what you've got", so it was all very there's the wall and we'll blast everything at it and try and find something that leads us in a direction.

(FD 6)

FD 6 explained the repercussions of this mindset to investigations, which perhaps illustrates how miscarriages of justice occurred during these times:

I think it was very flawed because what I think happened in [names homicide case] is then you start thinking "yes" and then particularly you've got defendants who have got criminal records, who are well known to the police, who are on the dark side of life and all of a sudden "yes it must be them and now what we'll try and do is prove it's them" and nobody had the reigns to draw people back and say "let's start investigating it from another area, another direction, let's forget about this group of people, what evidence is there?" It was cultural that kind of drive.

(FD 6)

FD 6 explained that to challenge the decisions of SIOs at this time would lead to you not being considered a team player, which would subsequently mean that you would not be selected to work on future enquiries:

I think the [names homicide case] is a good example that people are motivated, it's almost a testosterone pumped male culture that sometimes you think "hang on a second this needs somebody", but of course in the days that I'm talking about the 80s, 90s that person that stood out and said "hang on" you weren't seen as a team player, so very quickly wouldn't have been called onto the inquiries because you weren't a team player and you didn't actually see the world the way everyone else saw it.

(FD 6)

This might be considered an example of what Rossmo (2008, p. 176) calls "groupthink", a situation in which individuals are reluctant to "think critically and challenge the dominant theory". Rossmo (2008, p. 176) explains that "groupthink" often occurs amongst groups who are under pressure to make decisions and can therefore be applied to investigative work.

Although the literature surrounding the culture of detective work is scarce, what exists does reveal that detectives of the 1970s and 1980s would often "bend the rules". Maguire and Norris (1992, p. 21), for example, found that because their work was "unseen"; detectives could "sail close the wind" without significant repercussions (Maguire and Norris, 1992, p. 21). When we consider the way in which the SIO was perceived and the consequences to those who challenged their decisions, it is perhaps unsurprising that participants in this study reiterated this.

It must be acknowledged that the time periods of investigations that are at the centre of this research include those that preceded PACE and other pieces of legislation governing investigations and detective work. Therefore, a lot of what took place was not necessarily illegal in some instances as the legislation was not in existence. However, FD 5 explained how in one case there was an attempt to disregard PACE some five years after it was introduced, suggesting that it did not immediately correct practices:

> I was a custody officer in [names place] and we had a manslaughter, we had a lot of people who were involved in it, they had one person in custody that I was aware of, as the custody officer I was to be aware of everybody who was in the police station in custody or helping us with our inquiries, and I became aware that they had four other people in the CID office and I had no clue! This was '89 or something like that. Bloody stupid! "They're only helping us with our inquiries", "so why aren't they in this book then?" I went to the DI with that one because it was my responsibility.
>
> (FD 5)

Over 30 years later the comments made by many of those interviewed would suggest that the feared SIO seems consigned to history and the tunnel vision described above less likely today because of the way in which criminal investigations have been reformed:

> Much like the dinosaurs, Gene Hunt[6] went his way probably around the early to mid-1990s, he was gone.
>
> (SD 25)

If the feared SIO and the tunnel vision described here is no longer present, it is important to consider what was said about today's SIO and their approach to investigations. SD 8 explained that SIOs today are now focused on doing things right as opposed to just getting a result, a contrast to the comments of

---

6 DCI Gene Hunt was the main character in the aforementioned television series *Life on Mars* and *Ashes to Ashes*.

FD 1 who explained that in the past the focus was not "how you got there, it's if you got there":

> I think they've definitely changed. Now I like to think that they are smart people with compassion, emotional intelligence, soft skills, are really conscientious, want to do things right.
>
> (SD 8)

SD 23 also stressed the importance today of getting the right outcome as opposed to any outcome:

> It's about finding out what's happened and that might be proving what hasn't happened or proving somebody didn't do it as much as proving they did because I don't want to see the wrong person in prison.
>
> (SD 23)

SD 20 explained that the approach to investigations of the past would not be suitable today and believed that this was partly due to the fact that the world is a more diverse place:

> The world's more complex than it was when that was taking place, it wasn't as transient as it is now, you know, you look at the stats, I forget what they are now, but it's something like 70% of people will always live within five miles of where they are born, well that's changed and we've got communities that come in, Eastern European Labour markets and people return home at different periods, you've got all these added complexities of society, you've got different communities rubbing up against each other, communication barriers, all these things that are now taking place and it's no longer like policing a town where you could go into a pub and everyone knew who everyone was, all that's gone.
>
> (SD 20)

SD 20 worked for a large city police force, which might at least in part explain their views around the increasingly transient nature of communities today. However, the view that the approach to investigations that was evident during the 1970s and 1980s has no place in investigations today was echoed by other interviewees. SD 13, who worked for a smaller police force, explained that the culture was also partly due to the hierarchical nature of the police as an organisation and that there is now a deliberate move away from this. Crucially, in light of the above comments, this involves encouraging individuals to contest decision-making:

> People are actively encouraged to challenge decision-making by managers, we're losing that kind of hierarchical, we are a very hierarchical organisation and we are being encouraged to step away from that, there's definitely greater familiarity.
>
> (SD 13)

One example in which the changes in respect of culture that have been discussed here are apparent is when we consider the way in which briefings used to be run when compared to how they are led today. In particular, the changes to briefings reflect the changes in the SIO and how investigations are led. FD 11 explained that at the briefing at the start of the day the SIO would outline the important actions to be carried out and that:

> if you hadn't done the job you were humiliated in front of everyone else, so you came back with results or look out, you'd be kicked off the inquiry.
>
> (FD 11)

This illustrates the way in which SIOs at this time interacted with their teams. Although FD 11 denied that the fear of returning to the second briefing of the day without results led to poor practices, believing that it was key to identifying lazy detectives, it is possible to see how that might have been a risk. Briefings held during modern-day enquiries appear to be very different now and illustrate how the mindset towards investigations has shifted. SD 13 explained that in the early stages of an investigation they would be less of a two-way process and so would be more directed by the SIO, which is somewhat reminiscent of how the former detectives described briefings in the past:

> At those early stages the briefing is less two way and more directed from the front because you've got very little information at that stage and it's only beginning to unfold and the key thing is to make sure that all the team that you've got assembled are actually working on the things that are going to progress the investigation in the best way. Now every individual is going to have their own ideas about what they should be doing, but you really just need one person to say: "no this is what we are going to do".
>
> (SD 13)

However, he went on to explain that this would change as the investigation progressed:

> Then individuals would be holders of detailed information but only in one specific area and so the whole team perhaps needs to know that, so even though in the briefing, they're briefing me as the SIO at the same time they're briefing the rest of the team as well.
>
> (SD 13)

Although the complexities of investigations today are such that a two-way process of communication is necessary to ensure that the SIO and others are apprised of any developments, it is clear that they also indicate a wider change in how investigations are led and the culture of this work. This was also evident during the observations of briefings that I undertook. Indeed, one was filmed by a television crew for a documentary, and an SIO working for a large city police force explained that they allow students undertaking work experience to visit the MIR. This reflects an openness to investigations that was not apparent historically:

> Murder enquiries were closed events, they were closed events, you were in the murder inquiry room and you didn't talk about it outside that it was only the murder inquiry team that knew about it, it was only you that talked about it and nothing would be released outside, whereas there is a far more transparent view now, I hear that major incident rooms now are opening up to people to come in and out like yourself . . . and that's the way it should be.
>
> (FD 6)

Conclusion

In Chapter one I suggested that the first response that may come to mind as we consider the question "How have homicide investigations changed?" is scientific and technological advances. I proposed that this would likely be because of the media representations of crime that so often feature such techniques as being the key to solving the crime. What this chapter has shown, however, is that these techniques were also at the forefront of the detectives' minds as they reflected on the ways in which homicide investigations have changed "for the better". It is evident that now there are more lines of enquiry to pursue and that these tools allow detectives to paint a picture of what happened during a homicide. Throughout this chapter we have also considered other positive developments, including a move away from confession-oriented interviews to structured models of interviewing and apparent shifts in the broader detective culture. It has also been shown, however, that in many cases new opportunities have created new challenges that today's homicide detective, a detective who appears to bear little resemblance to their predecessor, must contend with. Questions have been raised about their ability to maintain pace with a fast-moving scientific and technological landscape and the possibility that models of interviewing are impeding investigators. Nevertheless, and whilst remaining mindful of the fact that the detectives might have been painting a positive image of their work to a researcher, it would appear that many of the changes that have taken place over the course of the past four decades have served to greatly improve the ways in which homicide investigations in England and Wales are currently conducted.

3 "It Can Be Easy Now to Forget That You've Got to Find the Actual Murderer"

Change and New Challenges

In the previous chapter it was shown how the changes that have taken place since the 1980s have presented those investigating homicide with new opportunities, most notably the developments in respect of science and technology but also improvements in interviewing practices and an apparent move away from a culture of feared SIOs. We also saw that these new opportunities have presented new challenges, such as those associated with managing the vast amount of information that investigations today generate. In this chapter we are continuing a consideration of the challenges that now face those investigating homicide, but our attention turns to some more overarching issues that were unearthed. In particular, we focus on the apparent risk aversion that appears to exist among today's homicide detectives and which appears to be a consequence of the changes that have been made over the years.

"I Do Think We've Become More Risk Averse": Bureaucracy, Risk Aversion and the Homicide Detective

The consequences of the focus on risk and the efforts to manage it appeared to be significant as risk aversion became a prominent theme as the research continued. In short, the issue of risk aversion became apparent when the interviewees discussed what they perceived to be an increase in bureaucracy. They explained that this has led to feelings of risk aversion; such are the consequences when "something goes wrong" during an investigation. This can be further understood when we take into account the view that the scrutiny that comes with a preoccupation with risk "carries with it the spectre of blame" (Kemshall, 2003, p. 12) and the need to hold someone to account when something goes wrong. It appears that increased legislation, regulation and guidance has led to a feeling that the police do "too much" when investigating homicide in order to "cover" themselves, due to the fear of the high-profile repercussions of making a mistake. FD 9

DOI: 10.4324/9781003201298-4

summarised this issue, explaining that the scrutiny and judgement that the police are subject to means that decisions and actions that are taken must be documented but that this bureaucracy has added to the volume of work that detectives must manage:

> I think the bureaucracy can sometimes get in the way and the volume of stuff, but I suppose we've become so judgemental on the way policing is developed that you've got to have stuff documented.
>
> (FD 9)

Today there are so many processes that they can seemingly be afraid to step outside of these processes and take a risk in case they are later criticised for doing so:

> Have we become risk averse? We probably have a society as police officers have been under investigation where criminal cases have been lost, there's always something to mould and chip away at policing and society, which in the main is a good thing but sometimes can be bureaucratic, cumbersome and psychologically force officers to take the path of least resistance.
>
> (SD 16)

SD 21 described a case, mentioned earlier in this book, that he considered to be an example of how risk aversion could manifest, explaining how SIOs could be afraid of not taking certain steps in case it is flagged up should a review take place:

> We had a murder where a guy killed his girlfriend, drove her into the police station, comes in the police station and says "I killed my girlfriend", even that inquiry was 7/8 months, hundreds of statements and actions and you think "well is that efficient?" and I mean you say there's no price on justice, but I do think well when you look at the public purse and staff resources and shortages, something like that surely should be a case of "right we're going to focus on this, he's saying he's killed her, we know he's killed her, there's no one else involved, he's saying he's had a moment of madness, well the experts can work around that" but no, we still, and a lot of that is SIO driven because they are afraid of that review because there's always someone that knows better, there's always "why didn't you do this, why didn't you do that, why didn't you get this expert?"
>
> (SD 21)

A QC offered a similar perspective. He also suggested that the police use a lot of resources pursuing red herrings because they feel that they have to do everything. Going back to the comments of SD 21, they too accepted that it would require a brave SIO to not take certain steps and acknowledged that care must be taken in case a suspect were to later change their story. However, they felt that each case should be looked at individually and managed accordingly rather than them practicing "policing by numbers":

> I think you've got to look at each one individually where we are guilty sometimes of having this checklist and you do have some SIOs who haven't got that detective background because that's the reality, you don't become an SIO through experience you attend a course, which is a bit odd really, so some will police by numbers as I say, it's like having a picture and they'll say right they'll have a chart of top 200 actions are this and they'll do, where I tend to think well each case I don't need to do, to get from a to z you don't always have to tick b,c,d,e,f, g, whereas some SIOs will be rigid, they're afraid of the review, afraid of the risk, not quite strong enough to policy things out and then you'll have a 10 month inquiry where perhaps you could have had a four month one.
>
> (SD 21)

One interviewee held the view that change needs to be proportionate and that the key thing for investigators is to know the fundamentals of what went wrong and what needs to be changed, as opposed to being overly "picky" and critical. The following comment from FD 9, who at the time of the interview had recently retired, illustrates how routine reviews of investigations need to be proportionate in the same way as enquiries into high-profile and problematic cases. Their comments suggest that increased bureaucracy in policing might prove detrimental to future investigations:

> What worries me sometimes is that we can sometimes lose sight of how many times something has gone right for one case that has gone wrong and we change the world for one case that has gone wrong and there may be a number of factors why that went wrong, so I think it's important to have some perspective on: does this really need to change? Was this just human error and mistakes? Because otherwise what we end up doing is creating a bureaucracy, which actually affects future investigations and can be detrimental.
>
> (FD 9)

The detectives felt that change often comes as a result of high-profile investigations that have been subject to criticism. In considering why this occurs, some of the interviewees' comments reflected the findings of Flanagan's (2008) "Review of Policing", that the government must be seen to be doing something in response to investigations that have been subject to criticism:

> A lot of this is driven from the top at Government level and, whichever Government, as soon as they get a sense of what the public attitude is towards something they will always want to be seen to be doing something. That's where it comes from and then be seen to say "right, this is what we've now put in place".
>
> (SD 13)

The result of this approach was that many significant changes are made in response to what is often an exceptional incident:

> We do an awful lot of those big changes in reaction to one isolated incident, which has gone horribly wrong, but that doesn't mean that everything has to be changed as a result.
>
> (SD 13)

However, there was certainly a sense amongst some interviewees that there are also benefits to an aversion to risk. SD 8 felt that the increased accountability that comes with increased risk aversion has made the police more intelligent in how they approach homicide investigations, and it is right that the police are held to account. This did not happen in the past:

> We are far more risk averse than we used to be, but I think that's a positive thing because I think we are far more responsible now, far more intelligent in our approach, far more accountable, rightly so, no-one used to challenge the police years ago.
>
> (SD 8)

Similarly, some interviewees were of the opinion that the changes that we have seen over the years mean that it is less likely that significant errors will occur. When asked whether we are likely to see future cases where miscarriages of justice have occurred, the majority of interviewees agreed that this would be very unlikely:

> I think we are in a far, far better position now to cover all the basis than what we ever were before.
>
> (FD 9)

Despite changes being made in respect of legislation and guidance, the question remains whether it is possible to prevent human error. During the interviews many detectives commented that mistakes will happen and that human error will occur despite the increased legislation, regulation and overall increased professionalisation of investigations. The interviewees often portrayed a sense of acceptance that, regardless of the changes that are made to investigations and scrutiny of the police, mistakes will be made and that they will often be the result of human error:

> That doesn't mean to say that we don't still make mistakes, when you're dealing with humans and people trying to do their best there's still always opportunity for error or to do something wrong or for something to be missed.
>
> (FD 9)

SD 25 also felt that human error would always be a factor in homicide investigations simply because of the nature of this work:

> I think there needs to be recognition that policing in general and detective work it's not a widget factory, we don't make 100 widgets a day Monday to Friday and if the machine goes wrong there's a few less widgets, our business is human misery, we deal with people in crisis, unpredictable events, strangely enough mistakes will be made.
>
> (SD 25)

The role of human error in problems that occur during homicide investigations has been discussed elsewhere. In their examination of 28-day homicide reviews, Nicol et al. (2004, p. 44) established that weaknesses or problems in investigations are often the result of:

> frailties in human processes, which make up so much of what constitutes an investigation: perceived poor judgement; inadequate knowledge; a failure to comply to agreed processes; an abrasive management style; and a lack of suitably trained personnel.

It is clear that changes that have occurred in respect of legislation, regulation and guidance for those investigating homicide in England and Wales have led to concerns that investigations are becoming increasingly bureaucratic, and detectives have perhaps become wary of stepping outside of the processes that have been implemented over the past few decades. At times when budgets are tight, the question of whether too much is done as detectives try to "cover" themselves becomes increasingly important.

"It's Right That We're Scrutinised": Legislation, Regulation and Guidance as Support

This chapter has so far outlined the challenges that have developed as a result of increased legislation, regulation and guidance that detectives investigating homicides must negotiate. Similarly, the literature suggests that such developments signalled a move "towards a more 'modern', rationalised and bureaucratic system" (Innes, 2003a, p. 24) and increased standardisation and professionalisation of investigations. It was certainly acknowledged that there had been positive outcomes from such shifts. Those that I spoke to agreed and commented that investigations of homicide were now more professional than they had been prior to the 1980s. This was evident in the recognition by many detectives, both former and serving, that we are unlikely to see the problems in homicide investigations that we saw historically.

In considering these changes, the detectives also spoke of how they have led to increased accountability, which was considered to be a positive development. They spoke of how homicide investigation is the most serious type of investigation because someone has lost their life and another will face a very long period of imprisonment; they therefore felt that it was right that they were now so accountable. This serving detective explained that as a result of past miscarriages of justice, there is distrust in the police, and so accountability is necessary:

> We don't do ourselves any favours. I mean the miscarriages of justice that have gone on in the past, people don't believe the cops unreservedly anymore, years ago they did and we could get away with planting evidence, burying evidence, the Kiscko's of this world, the Guildford bombers, and we should be scrutinised. We are dealing with the most serious of offences and putting people in prison for the rest of their lives, that's a massive responsibility and therefore the decisions that led to that should be scrutinised, we should be accountable to the public. It's probably our transgressions of the past that have led to distrust.
>
> (SD 15)

The detectives held similar views on the increased levels of scrutiny, believing it to be necessary due to the seriousness of the offence. This is reflected in the comments of SD 20, who also explained that increased scrutiny, such as from the then Independent Police Complaints Commission (IPCC), comes as a consequence of the government wanting to improve the standard of investigations:

> You've got the IPCC taking a more fundamental role, there's a real concerted assertion from the Government to raise standards in policing,

so that brings with it more scrutiny and, to be fair, there should be more scrutiny around these investigations, it's right that we are scrutinised.
(SD 20)

SD 20 also felt that because of the scrutiny to which homicide investigations are subject, the standards of investigations are very high, particularly when compared to other countries that do not experience such levels of scrutiny:

One of the things that you can rely on is that British justice will 9 times out of 10 times, give you that certainty that when you've got your man, you've got your man because of the layers of assessment and scrutiny that they go through. If you think of a system that's far less stable than ours, look at American standards, and, their cops are allowed to lie, in certain states it's different of course, but in some states their cops can interview someone and tell them lies to illicit confessions and the difference is that the majority of their jobs come as a result of confessions whereas the majority of results of our jobs come as a result of evidence, so if that's not a better standard, I don't know what is.
(SD 20)

Arguably, it could be deduced from the data that the positive view of these changes explain why the detectives felt that they were now receptive to reform:

Legislation has come in place for good reason and people have got on with it and, by and large, people now are as flexible as they ever were.
(FD 12)

It is undeniable that the changes that have been made to the regulation of homicide investigations in England and Wales have been positive in many respects. Nevertheless, the detectives appeared to hold a somewhat ambivalent view of the changes that have been made; they could see its necessity but still expressed some concerns.

Risk Aversion: Taking a Step Back

It is important here to consider what bureaucracy means. In this context bureaucracy refers to the processes and procedures that now make up a significant part of the investigative process and which appear to be an added source of pressure and additional work. Although there are certainly positive aspects to bureaucracy as was outlined above, the detectives often spoke of it with negative connotations attached and in ways that indicated that it was a burden to them. For example, they described the layers of bureaucracy involved when examining a suspect's phone, which could take a considerable amount of time. A similar perspective is evident in the research of Westera et al. (2016) in their study exploring the challenges to detectives being effective in the future. Based on research conducted in Australia and New Zealand, they also found that detectives were concerned about increasing bureaucratic processes that have been implemented in a bid to ensure accountability, avoid risk and measure performance (Westera et al., 2016).

Issues of risk and bureaucracy were identified in 2008 when the aforementioned review of policing was requested by the then Home Secretary in response to concerns that policing had become overly bureaucratic. Led by Sir Ronnie Flanagan, it "identified risk aversion as a primary cause of bureaucratic processes" (Heaton, 2011, p. 79). The report identified two triggers that impact upon the way in which processes have been designed:

1. Internally – a "just in case" mentality, which leads to every process being designed to the worst case scenario without regard to how it will be handled by thousands of officers on a day to day basis.
2. Externally – a public approach, vocalised by the media and politicians that this "must never happen again" – which results in the same outcome.

(Flanagan, 2008, p. 52)

This suggests that risk aversion across the police service leads to the implementation of top-down bureaucratic procedures. However, the detectives that I spoke to explained that these bureaucratic procedures have made *them* increasingly risk averse and spoke of being nervous of stepping away from the processes. Thus, it seems that the response to the police service's aversion to risk has created risk aversion amongst those directly affected by new procedures. In a further indication of the prevalence of risk, the report also states, "Over recent years we have started to see an even more insidious extension: the expectation that the service should have anticipated events and incidents that are well beyond their control" (Flanagan, 2008, p. 52).

Turnell, Munro and Murphy (2013, p. 200) write of similar responses to the deaths of children who were known to social services, with the phrase "lessons will be learned" often dominating discussions. With minimal literature concerning these issues in respect of the investigation of homicide, it is again useful here to briefly consider what the literature around responses to child deaths can tell us. Munro (2010, p. 1146) draws on the work of Hood, Rothstein and Baldwin (2001) in arguing how one response to reducing risk in child protection is that of "introducing more and more detailed formal procedures setting out the 'correct' way to deal with a case in steps that can be readily performed and measured". This is reminiscent of the steps that have been taken towards professionalising investigations and in response to miscarriages of justice, such as the introduction of the Murder Investigation Manual (MIM), as discussed in Chapter one. Further, Munro (2010, p. 1146) writes that the purpose of such an approach allows the "defence of 'due diligence' if a tragic outcome occurs. Senior management can demonstrate how their staff followed all correct procedures in working with the case and therefore cannot be blamed".

This stance is reflected in the findings from my research, which illustrated that detectives will make reference to documents such as the then MIM within homicide case files to support decisions that were made. Specifically, despite the fact that the SIOs questioned how beneficial the document is, the defence will have access to it, and according to one detective, they may ask why certain procedures were not followed:

If you go to Crown Court they might pick you up on it.

(SD 8)

The importance of showing reference and adherence to the MIM and explaining why certain decisions were made was reflected in the homicide case file from the 2000s that was examined. In explaining the decisions that were taken around the Community Impact Assessment, it states "compliance with good practice/murder manual" (2000s Homicide Case File). Additionally, the same case file notes that the set-up of the MIR "reflects MIRSAP recommendations" (2000s homicide case file). On the one hand, this suggests that a degree of importance is attached to such guidance despite the issues that have been discussed here; on the other, this is a further indication that the police are increasingly risk averse as regulation increases and feel it is necessary to try and "cover" themselves in this way even though the MIM is a guidance document and not enshrined in law. This arguably links to the concept of defensible decision-making. Carson (1996), as cited by Kemshall (2009, p. 333), defined defensible decisions as those "that will withstand the harsh scrutiny of hindsight bias in the event of risk failure". The notion of defensible decision-making during homicide investigations is evident in earlier research. Maguire and Norris (1992, p. 66) revealed that detectives had been sceptical about the introduction of the policy book, fearing that it would be used to "hammer them into the ground when the inquiry went wrong". However, despite this initial scepticism, they came to see the positives of its introduction as it "made the SIOs think more carefully about their decisions and the justifications for them. If the decisions turned out to be wrong, as long as the justification was rational there was no cause for recriminations" (Maguire and Norris, 1992, p. 66).

More than 20 years after Maguire and Norris' (1992) research, it is clear that whilst documenting decisions remains useful for SIOs, the point that a strong rationale will mean that there are no recriminations should errors be made is no longer certain, since it is these elements of an investigation that might be the focus of the defence:

> Adherence to procedural requirements and justification of policy deci-
> sions are usually what an SIO gets cross-examined on in court proceed-
> ings (i.e. also known as "trial by policy decision"), whereas historically
> cross-examination used to focus upon the honesty and integrity of
> detectives' activities and behaviour.
>
> (Cook and Tattersall, 2010, p. 18)

This is something that was reported by the detectives in this research. How-ever, the QC reported that in his experience, it was unlikely that this would be a major focus of the defence, but he had also found that this is something that detectives are particularly nervous about. Munro (2010, p. 1147) also argues that the defence of due diligence, whilst helpful for the individual as it is their "cover", will lead them to "opt for the safer route of follow-ing procedures, however inappropriate they may seem in a particular case". This brings us to the delicate balance between detectives using individual skills and initiative whilst ensuring that they are working in accordance with the relevant legislation and guidance. The findings of the literature outlined above mirror the detectives' views that bureaucracy will lead risk-averse detectives to take the path of least resistance. This raises the question of whether the tendencies of some detectives to rigidly follow processes might impact upon their ability to successfully investigate hard-to-solve homicides, or what Innes (2003a) terms "whodunits", where detective skills are seen to be particularly crucial.

Kemshall (2003) writes that the use of systems and audits in controlling risk replaces trust in professionals. This somewhat corresponds with the Home Office research on increased bureaucracy in policing, which found that new processes are often implemented because of a "just in case" men-tality (Flanagan, 2008). It is perhaps unsurprising that my findings illustrate a reluctance by individuals to step outside of those processes because of the resulting risk aversion. This is despite the fact that the SIO handbook stresses that "creativity and innovations" should be encouraged and that "finding legal solutions to legal problems is a key skill for an SIO" (Cook and Tattersall, 2010, p. 12). It could therefore be argued that there exists a tension between using creativity and following processes that is potentially exacerbated by aversion to risk. There is, however, evidence to the contrary. Innes (2003a) found that although homicide detectives placed a significant degree of importance upon scientific and technological tools, the art and craft elements of detective work were apparent when they were investigating more complex cases. On these occasions they would adopt innovative and creative approaches.

The disparity in the findings of the present research and that of Innes (2003a) might be attributed to the 14-year gap between them as the concerns mentioned by the former and serving detectives in my research are evident in more recent work. Examining the role of flair in major crime investigation, Fox (2014, p. 13) also found that some detectives viewed the MIM as providing a "prescriptive list of activities" that had to be followed. Further, he found that "several respondents held the view that the existence of national police guidance might create a 'tick box' mentality or even risk averse mentality amongst police investigators" (Fox, 2014, p. 13). Fox (2014) acknowledges that this was not the intention of such guidance but that these findings resonate with those that I uncovered. The matters discussed here might be linked with what Brookman and Innes (2013, p. 2) term "procedural accountability", whereby "detectives can demonstrate to others (both inside and outside the police) their compliance with official guidance". Their work exploring what constitutes a successful homicide investigation identified four definitions of success, including "procedural success": "compliance with legal procedures and official guidance was a prominent feature of detective talk and the ways in which they explained and justified many of the decisions they took" (Brookman and Innes, 2013, p. 9).

Explorations of organisational behaviour suggest that history has an impact upon the way in which decisions are made, which may help to explain some of the ways in which decisions are now made during an investigation since the police service have been heavily criticised over the years for the way in which numerous homicides were investigated: "decisions aren't made in a vacuum; they have a context. Individual decisions are points in a stream of choice, those made in the past are like ghosts that haunt and constrain current choices" (Robbins and Judge, 2008, p. 121). Risk aversion might be a consequence of detectives being aware of times in the past when things have gone wrong, leading to enquiries and major change. This might be making them overly cautious in their conduct lest they make a mistake and become the subject of a future enquiry and the focus of the significant media attention that would undoubtedly follow. Indeed, it is telling that many of those interviewed in the present research stressed that despite the increased regulation of investigative work, it would never fully eradicate human error. Relatedly, they felt that it is important to maintain perspective when errors are made and in ensuring that any subsequent change is approached with caution. The introduction of increased legislation and guidance has, in many respects, been helpful to those investigating homicide in England and Wales. However, responses to high-profile and highly criticised cases clearly warrant review, for they raise questions around the proportionality of responses. This has been considered in respect of major accidents. Hutter and Lloyd-Bostock (1990) found that major accidents generate significant changes whilst more routine errors are often overlooked. Similarly, Innes (2003a) explains that actions that could be deemed "compliance drift" are often overlooked with focus being upon major failings in criminal investigations. What we have seen here is that increased bureaucracy is continuing to create pressure for detectives, and it might be argued that this could lead to the bypassing of procedures that could, in turn, culminate in an increase in serious failings in major crime investigations.

Doing More With Less

> We are expected to do much more with less and inquiries now bring lines of enquiry, which even 10 years ago weren't even thought of, so resources is probably the biggest issue.

(SD 15)

Carson (2007, p. 408) writes that "[the idea that] justice might have a price tag or budget offends popular sensibilities and is rarely highlighted in academic discourse about criminal justice", and so whilst the idea of discussing budget in relation to homicide in particular may seem uncomfortable, the cuts to police budgets mean that it is a necessary consideration. Although caution must be urged, as specific costs will depend upon the circumstances of the offence, the advent of scientific and technological tools will impact upon the cost of police investigations of homicide. To give some idea as to the monetary impact of such tools, during a presentation given by an SIO that I attended as part of the fieldwork, it was noted that sending just one exhibit for forensic testing could cost around £2,500. Similarly, the homicide case file from the 1990s reveals the budgetary demands that forensics can create. In this case the victim was reported missing in the mid-1990s, but the remains were not found until the late 2000s. The case file notes that forensic expense after the discovery of the body was £26,000 and notes that there is an initial cap on Category A investigations of £50,000. However, budget is not something that would have been a central concern for the detective of the past as the data reveal a sense that money would be very much "thrown at" a homicide investigation:

> With [names case] they threw money at it. I would come on duty at 6 o'clock in the morning to get to [names place] for 7 o'clock and then back on at 6 o'clock the next day, which went on day after day and you're talking 18 hours overtime for all those people for all those days and we worked rest days because they cancelled rest days, but no one batted an eyelid because it was important and had to be done, nowadays you would be "who's on rest days, who's not on rest days" and all that would be taken into account.
>
> (FD 4)

Although this observation does not refer to any forensic or technological costs, which would not have been prevalent at the beginning of the 1980s, it does illustrate the general attitude towards homicide budgets of the past. Again, this was evident in the case files where there was little mention of budget in the 1980s investigation. Evidence of a change in perspective regarding budgets is reflected in the following extract taken from the SIO policy file relating to the 1990s homicide mentioned above. The victim's body was eventually found in the late 2000s, and the following extract demonstrates the SIO's thoughts on forensics at the time that the remains were discovered in the 2000s. It should be noted that there was no mention of budget in the file that was produced in the 1990s, which may be due to there being less emphasis on budget at the time but also likely because it was a missing persons case with no body; therefore, there was no opportunity for forensic work to be carried out:

> The forensic spend is clearly significant and will increase as these additional submissions are made. This is a very high profile and important investigation and I believe every forensic opportunity to identify an offender should be pursued.
>
> (1990s Homicide Case File)

There was also a sense that difficult decisions had to be made in respect of what forensic exhibits are or are not sent off for testing because of budget considerations. This too was evident in the 1990s case. The SIO who was appointed following the discovery of the victim's remains in the late 2000s writes that what has been spent in relation to forensics has been "necessary and proportionate" (1990s Homicide Case File). This is further indication that SIOs are increasingly mindful of budget. The following comment summarises how the police manage the obvious need for testing of exhibits with this mindfulness of budget:

> We make a decision early on, say on forensics you may have 1,000 items that you can send off to analyse, but is that proportionate for what you are trying to achieve? So you sit down and have a forensic management meeting, you'll sit down with your crime scene advisor, the SIO, the exhibits officer and you will come up with a plan, if you like, for phased, you may phase your submissions, so if you have the culprit's fingerprints at the scene, do you need 30 of his fingerprints at the scene? So you will achieve the evidential standard in the least expenditure.
>
> (SD 15)

Whilst this appears to be a logical approach to the way in which scientific and technological evidence and budgets are managed, SD 23, who works for a different police service, suggested that there can be conflict between the SIO and those responsible for the budget:

> I've never scrimped on resourcing, but I have had to go into some real battles along the way with budget holders. Because I don't hold the budget for forensics, I don't hold a budget for telecoms, I don't hold the budget for external technology providers, so I will ask for that stuff to be carried out or those things to be done, but I will have to lock horns along the way with budget holders.
>
> (SD 23)

One former detective emphasised also that budget is something that SIOs have to be mindful of and stressed the importance of SIOs writing clear policies and strategies around this in order that they will withstand scrutiny. This is important when we consider that defence barristers may ask questions around why certain exhibits were or were not sent off for examination:

> That's not saying that money is the first thing we think about but we have got a limited budget, so we've got to be more realistic about what we can do and the more precise SIOs can get with these policies and strategies of what really needs to be done that means that everything comes together and we get the right outcome and that outcome will stand the test of time and the reviews and scrutiny and everything else.
>
> (FD 9)

Fundamentally, the interviewees stressed that the issue of money is not something that would hinder an investigation and that investigators would never be told that they could not have additional money, as the quote below from a former detective who continues to work within major crime investigation shows:

> We've lost staff and people have lost their jobs as a result of the issues that are around at the moment, so we are always conscious of finance but on homicide nobody has ever said to me "you cannot have that analysed because of money".
>
> (SD 15)

Nevertheless, budget is clearly something that the current detectives are mindful of. This leads us to consider the view of some that the availability of science and technology in investigations could lead investigators to go too wide in their efforts to ensure that everything is covered and everything is collected, reinforcing the view that there needs to be an awareness of budgets and proportionality. The following quote illustrates the importance of this and shows that there are such cases in which investigators will indeed go too wide "just in case":

> I think there should always be those checks and balances and the person who holds the purse strings in this force will always say "in theory this is no limit to the amount of money you can spend on this investigation but you need to convince me there is a purpose or potential there" and in my experience some SIOs do go off at tangents and think "well I'll get this done because in my head this might possibly lead to a very peripheral, association to the crime" but going back to pragmatism and what is realistic, we can't do everything all the time.
>
> (FD 27)

In summary, it is clear that those interviewed did not feel budgetary restrictions proved to be a hindrance to investigations. At the same time, investigators are conscious of the cost that scientific and technological tools and evidence can bring, which can sometimes lead to difficult discussions to be held with those responsible for budget and careful decisions to be made in respect of what evidence is tested. As we saw in Chapter one, police budgets continue to face cuts, and so such difficult decisions will surely endure.

Just a Job?

According to the interviewees, to be a detective during the 1970s, 1980s and early 1990s carried with it a degree of kudos. Detectives at this time were seen as being different to other police officers, as "something special".

They described how detectives were considered to know a lot and were perceived as being more expert than others. Detectives were also said to be the most likely to take risks, which has been identified by others (Hobbs, 1988; Maguire and Norris, 1992). SD 16, who joined the police service in 1994, described being a uniformed officer going into the CID office as "daunting" and explained that there was an "air of superiority" and an "us and them" relationship between the uniformed officers and those in CID. Such phrasing is demonstrative of both the kudos that detectives carried and of the impression that they were set apart from everyone else:

> Because you were a detective you'd carry a bit of kudos with you.
>
> (FD 1)

However, the majority of detectives, both former and serving, reported that this kudos no longer exists. According to one interviewee the detective is now viewed as being no more or less important than a uniformed police officer, suggesting also that the divide between uniformed officers and detectives is no longer apparent:

> You are not seen as something different anymore, you are just a policeman in plainclothes.
>
> (FD 4)

On the other hand, some felt that this kudos remained. When speaking to two serving detectives informally between interviews they suggested that it remained because of the work and effort that they had put into becoming detectives and that this set them apart from those in uniform. This was later discussed during an interview with one of these individuals, who was a junior SIO. He explained that being a detective and wearing plain clothes showed that they were elite:

> I worked for my D. [Not wearing a uniform] is our badge of eliteness.
>
> (SD 14)

Nevertheless, the dominant view was that the kudos no longer existed. Some felt that other areas of policing now carried kudos and that there was an equal amount of status for those working in the firearms department, for example. Others suggested that there is more awareness of detective work now, and so the mystery that used to surround this work is no longer evident. As the interviews continued it became increasingly apparent that the status of the detective has changed and the way that the detectives themselves view their position has shifted significantly; this became apparent as the phrase "just a job" was repeated. It was suggested that for younger officers today to be a detective is merely seen as "just a job" and not perhaps seen to be the calling that it was for those working during the 1970s, 1980s and early 1990s:

> I think it's the same type of breed of people. I think that perhaps what has gone now is the yearning of some people, they don't have the calling anymore they see it as just a job, people join the police service as a job, I mean I never thought I'd ever say that but people do, they don't see this as a service they're doing to a society or something they feel that they want to do, it's a job.
>
> (FD 1)

One interviewee outlined the benefits of the "job for life" ethos that used to exist. FD 6 suggested that the vocational nature of detective work engendered a commitment to the role, and detectives would work very long hours without being concerned by overtime:

> It was something about the vocational work that gave you commitment and drive, you worked long hours, you'd come in at 8 o'clock in the morning and if you were still there at 8 o'clock at night you wouldn't question it, you wouldn't say "I need the overtime", it was just done as part of the job.
>
> (FD 6)

These comments do provide us with an indication as to what might have been the impact of this shift in ethos. Specifically, it suggests that there has been a loss of commitment to the role, with more emphasis upon working hours and pay. Indeed, one serving detective suggested that those joining the police service today are mindful of the fact that they have to pay off university fees and so are looking for something that will provide them with a stable income:

> I think it goes back to society and we, as the police, recruit from society and as detectives we recruit from the police and the pay that constables get now is pretty horrific, but a lot of people come out of university, they need a job that's a steady income to pay off their fees and they don't see it as "this is something that I'm going to be doing for 30 years" they see it as "I've got to earn this money".
>
> (SD 24)

In considering the reasons why there has been a shift from a "job for life" to "just a job" mindset, many of those interviewed suggested that there is an increasing desire amongst individuals to try and achieve a "work life" balance. However, it is clear that the work required of a detective does not lend itself to achieving a "work life" balance due to the unpredictable working hours, particularly during the initial stages of a murder investigation:

> The first 3–4 days can be utter madness, then I say you're working through, working through means from 7/8 in the morning to when it finished at night time, which can be 11/12, you're working through most days and I'd say right through whatever rest days, you know, 7–10 days right on the trot on the first start of a murder.
>
> (SD 24)

It also became clear that the police are experiencing difficulties in recruiting detectives, suggesting perhaps that the role has changed to such an extent that individuals no longer wish to pursue it. Difficulties in recruiting detectives were reportedly being experienced by five of the seven English and Welsh forces that formed the sample for this research. SD 25 told of there being 15 vacancies for detectives in their police force but a lack of applicants, something that, according to one serving detective who joined the police service in the 1980s, would not have been a concern then:

> Years ago you'd be filling dead men's shoes.
>
> (SD 18)

The issue of recruitment has been recognised elsewhere (HMIC, 2017). When asked why police services were struggling to recruit detectives, many interviewees appeared at a loss to explain it. However, the following comment demonstrates how the role of the detective was viewed in the early 1990s and which may have a bearing on the challenges with recruitment. As a serving detective with 24 years' service, SD 8 talks about why he wanted to become a detective. The reasons given are linked to the kudos and culture that was associated with the position. This might explain why, with a loss of kudos and a change in detective culture, there are now issues with recruitment:

> In my day it was more about being a detective, because when you had someone escape from prison the CID would come on at four o'clock in the morning smashing every door in the street causing absolute mayhem getting control of an estate and they'd catch the person and it was great and then by 11 or 12 o'clock they'd be playing snooker and they'd be drinking and it was that type of culture and the youngsters wanted to be a part of that gang because they wouldn't, half of them wouldn't carry

a radio, they were rebels really, they were sent all over the force to do different jobs and for me I used to look and think I need to be a part of that and I did everything I could to be a part of it, they had the best jobs, that's how I saw it, you know, they chased the best people, they arrested the best people, they were allocated the best work, . . . I found it really exciting the prospect of being part of that team you know.

(SD 8)

Another explanation was that there are other factors that inform an individual's decisions in deciding whether or not to become a detective today, such as the working hours required and the pay, as was discussed previously. SD 24 explained that whilst a uniformed officer is required to work shifts, which they acknowledged brings its own challenges, they will receive a quite significant shift allowance, which a detective would not. Additionally, SD 24 suggested that whilst the uniformed officer has to work their ten-hour shift, once that is over, they can go home, whereas she explained that when the detective goes home, they are still thinking about what work needs to be done:

One of the things that's very prominent is the fact that nowadays if you are a uniformed police officer you are on shifts, which is horrible but you get quite a significant shift allowance, which is thousands of pounds more than a detective with less, I would say, responsibility long term. Although they have responsibility for ten hours where they've got to keep everybody safe and do the job and answer everything, but at the end of the ten hours they say "thanks very much" and go home, whereas detectives wake up at two o'clock going "oh my god I haven't done that". Nobody wants that responsibility with less money.

(SD 24)

SD 25 suggested that the pressures that the organisation are facing more broadly, such as cuts, are damaging the "mojo" of the police, which will in turn lead individuals to be reluctant to join the police and reluctant to progress through the ranks:

We are a-political and we are not allowed to have a view on politics, but it does feel like under this current [Conservative] government that there has been outright hatred for the police, it is barely concealed from my point of view . . . they have knocked the stuffing out of us and I am not sure how we will get it back, us as an organisation have taken an absolute kicking over the last five years and I think that general the confidence and gusto of what we had before that made us successful is gone and I find that really frustrating.

(SD 25)

Looking forward, SD 24 suggested that the problems around recruitment might have a detrimental impact in years to come:

> I think having a lack of people wanting to come into the detective world, a lack of experience in investigating major crimes and every-thing around that, I think that's going to have a knock on effect in the future, I may not see it, but it's going to have a huge knock on effect and if you did your . . . your PhD, a review of it in eight years, ten years' time you might find a poor situation in relation to it.
>
> (SD 24)

At this point it is relevant to consider what the detectives that I spoke to thought about the increased use of civilian investigators in the investigation of major crime as one of the ways in which the police service is attempt-ing to tackle the issue of detective recruitment involves the introduction of direct entry for detectives. One serving detective noted that only 23% of the staff that made up the MCIT in this force were detectives and the rest of the team were civilian staff. When asked why there has been a move towards the use of civilian staff in the investigation of homicide, many remarked that it is a change aimed at saving money:

> In our force we've had to lose £40 million in four years and we'll have to lose I think £40 million in the next 4 years, and staff costs are the greatest costs, so police officer numbers have reduced dramatically.
>
> (SD 22)

The civilians employed to work within major crime investigations come from a variety of backgrounds, with different experiences and skill sets, and are cheaper to employ. SD 22 described the civilian staff within their MCIT as a "complete and utter mixed bag". SD 13, who worked for the same police service, reiterated this:

> Some were ex-police officers, but not all, some had come straight in from university, some from other investigative type roles, like insur-ance investigators, it's pretty much 50/50 in terms of investigators that we would put on outside action teams, we've probably got 28 DCs and a similar number of what we call Major Crime Investigation Officers.
>
> (SD 13)

In considering the implications of civilians working on homicide investigation, one interviewee was critical of their use in running HOLMES. FD 12 was a retired detective now working as a HOLMES document reader/ receiver. He suggested that there might be problems in the future when the retired detectives, who often return to the police service as civilian staff, have gone and it is only those without a police investigative background working on HOLMES. FD 12 felt strongly that experience of detective work is an important part of being able to efficiently run the system:

> There is no investigative background . . . I think to do those roles, they're not an administrative role, they are first and foremost investigators as part of the investigation team and the danger is that they will be purely civilianised.
>
> (FD 12)

SD 13 also spoke of the difficulties that can be associated with civilians working within MIRs, such as occasions whereby alibis were not followed up. However, SD 13 also remarked that there are enough experienced individuals working within that team, including former police officers, that any problems should be swiftly identified. SD 22, who works for the same police service as SD 13, where civilians make up a significant percentage of their team, gave another example of such issues:

> To me that's where we've lost that basic policing investigative skill and a lot of our police staff do, for example, roles like the Exhibits Officer, which a lot of people presume is a case of just cataloguing the exhibits, but it's not, you need to interpret them. And a great example, the murder on Christmas Day, we didn't know when he had died and in the exhibits there was a receipt for a burger bar from the 16th December so ten days earlier or something, and they didn't even consider it, they just logged it, probably put a photocopy into the MIR for somebody else to review later. Now, as it transpires the victim was actually murdered on the 17th so suddenly that became very significant but, by the time we realised that, the CCTV from the burger bar had gone, so my question was "well why didn't you, when you looked at that consider . . . because not even around the murderer, but a potential witness, getting the CCTV so we could at least have a line of enquiry from the witness?" "Oh I don't know". So you have to try and instil investigative detective skills in somebody who hasn't had that basic upbringing from shoplifters to car thefts to burglars to assaults to kidnap or whatever other crimes.
>
> (SD 22)

Those who seemed most critical of the use of civilians in homicide investigations were often former officers themselves, some of whom were now working as police staff. They placed much importance on investigative experience and were concerned about those without such experience working on investigations. Their views might therefore be a reflection of their own experiences and the time at which they were serving, a time before civilian investigators perhaps. Conversely, one serving detective argued that whether or not an individual held a warrant card made no difference to their abilities as it was what they could bring to the investigation that was more important. They argued that no one is born a detective and that everyone has to learn and gain experience in this line of work, which can be achieved by civilians. When asked how someone learns to be a detective, they responded that it was down to training and experience, notably exposure to cases:

> It matters not whether you are a cop or a civilian, it's the training and how you get there that's important.
>
> (SD 15)

Furthermore, one serving detective argued that there are important traits required of investigators that might be possessed by any individual. Indeed, when others were asked what skills were required to be an "effective detective" (Smith and Flanagan, 2000), the traits mostly cited were being resilient or dogged.

None of the interviewees reported the presence of civilians in investigations that they worked on in the 1970s, 1980s or 1990s, and there was no reference to them in the homicide case files that were reviewed. When speaking informally to one detective between interviews about the future of homicide investigation, they suggested that it would see increased numbers of civilian staff. If the concerns of those interviewed for this research are correct, the mounting employment of civilian staff raises questions for the future efficiency of homicide investigations. These issues become increasingly important when we consider that exposure to investigations as part of training is becoming increasingly difficult.

Learning on the Job Versus Learning in the "Classroom"

Historically, the training of detectives was delivered through a detective training course, a programme of continual training that was delivered over a ten-week period (Tong, 2009)[1]. The former detectives and several long-term

---

1 This training period was reduced to six weeks in the 1990s (Tong, 2009). The interviewees' who discussed training spoke only of the ten-week course.

serving detectives spoke of undertaking this training. Although other areas were covered, such as forensic issues and how to present at court, some felt that the training did not cover other important elements of investigation and was mostly focused on the law. Since the feeling amongst many was that the training focused upon the law and, according to some, did not prepare them for the reality of this work, the question then arose: how do detectives learn to conduct investigations?

The detectives felt strongly that it was learning from others. FD 2 explained that this was particularly essential as he did not undertake the ten-week detective training until sometime after joining the CID:

> People you work with, all of your peers, it's on the job, simple as. I joined the CID in January 1982 and I did my course May of '83.
>
> (FD 2)

The comment above is particularly telling since he did not consider the training to have been helpful despite the fact that he would have had some investigation experience before attending. Although no other detectives told of having to wait to attend the course, all reiterated the importance of learning from others. The following comment illustrates the importance that many placed upon this even though on occasion the advice being given was not necessarily useful:

> Experience is key to it because you will come across things you've never dealt with before therefore if you've got experience of somebody else who's been there, even if what they're telling you is a load of old rubbish, you still know a little bit about it don't you?
>
> (FD 10)

Whilst the detectives expressed that learning from colleagues was a fundamental part of training in the past, it was not simply the case that they would take on board everything that they witnessed or were told. Several interviewees explained that they would take on board some things that they observed and disregard others:

> You worked with lots of different people and you looked at how they operated and how they investigated; attending scenes, interviewing people, speaking to witnesses and ultimately you take on board the things that you like off people, then you jettison things that you don't like. And you also look at what works and what doesn't work.
>
> (FD 1)

This comment is interesting in several respects. As well as again revealing the importance that was placed on learning from others, it is also reflective of the craft model (Stelfox, 2009) of investigations that was particularly evident in the 1970s, 1980s and 1990s. The comments of FD 1 also raises the question of how a junior detective would know what was considered good and bad practice, and so what to "jettison"?

The approach to the training of detectives was to change considerably in the mid-2000s with the introduction of the PIP, which was to provide a standardised and professionalised approach to training and a way of measuring the competency of investigators (Stelfox, 2009). Introduced in September 2005, its establishment was described by SD 20 as a significant development, particularly the recognition that certain skills were required to investigate murder, which they felt detective training lacked historically:

> For me the watershed moment would be making sure you're PIP accredited. The distinction I would make between before that time is the understanding that murder required an assessment of your skills or portfolio. To make sure you're qualified is a sea-change to times in the past where you wouldn't necessarily look on that as a necessary component to investigate murder.
>
> (SD 20)

During the fieldwork I attended SIO training and observed that PIP appears to have retained elements of training from the past. Part of the training involved a former Crown Prosecution Service lawyer attending and taking the attendees through the process of applying for a warrant for further detention. This involved a role-play format, and each attendee went through the application with the lawyer. Afterwards the group were given feedback on their performance and general tips on attendance at court. This indicates that the legal aspects of investigation understandably remain an important part of the training process and that this is delivered in such a way as to recreate situations that the detectives will face. Additionally, a forensic expert attended and advised participants. They described the history of DNA and discussed other important issues, such as avoiding the contamination of evidence.

Referring to the training of SIOs, FD 2 explained that the structure today is designed to put them under pressure and that this is achieved, suggesting that the conditions of the training today are designed to be more reflective of the situations in which they will find themselves. This would indicate that the training has addressed the concerns discussed above since the practical element now comprises a significant component of modern-day training:

> You act as an SIO for a week in a training room environment and you lead it and it's a system which has been developed to put you under pressure and test you and you do get that.
>
> (FD 2)

PIP also provides a way in which to measure the competency of detectives. Following the training and time that is then spent in the workplace to apply what has been learnt, officers are assessed against National Occupational Standards (Stelfox, 2009). This is something that, according to the interviewees, was not catered for previously. The importance and emphasis placed upon measuring the competency of detectives today can also be linked to the comments of FD 2. Whilst accepting that the training today is more focussed, FD 2 explained how the professionalisation and standardisation of training today provides a way for the police service to cover themselves if something were to go wrong during an investigation:

> There is an element of, excuse the term, backside covering now. We're always open to litigation now, so if we get it wrong it's always in the media so you have to make sure that the training has been delivered, that it covers the areas, so that if it ever comes to that it goes wrong, there's inquests or litigation of some sort at least you know the officer has received the right level of training.
>
> (FD 2)

Overall, it was apparent that most interviewees deemed the training today to be an improvement upon that which was delivered until the mid-2000s. However, given the importance that was placed upon experience "on the job" and learning from others in the past, the pertinent question that remained in considering the data on training today was whether it is this or classroom learning that is key to preparing detectives for modern-day homicide investigation. It would appear that the answer is that it was experience and learning whilst "on the job" that was considered to be the most effective form of training, something also identified by Smith and Flanagan (2000). This was a view that was held by all of the interviewees:

> There is no training like on the job training.
>
> (SD 18)

> Experience is key.
>
> (FD 10)

SD 14 felt particularly that learning on the job and having a broad experience of homicide investigations was key to becoming an effective SIO. It is worth noting here that at the time of the interview, SD 14 had yet to take part in the three-week SIO training course, which might explain his views:

> It's learning from what you do, from the job and it's work experience. If I took a layperson off the street, a very intelligent person like yourself,

and gave you a 3 or 4 week SIO course and then sent you to SIO a murder, I would probably do it better – through life and work experience rather than sitting down and taking a front loaded course.

(SD 14)

SD 14 explained that although he was a relatively junior SIO, his 18-year background in policing has meant that he has been exposed to, and been involved with, murder investigations for some time:

I've been involved in murder investigations in various roles since, the first one was in 1998. I've been on the periphery, the action team, I've office managed a murder, so I know how the system works. So it's a case of you've got the experience of policing in general to have the capability.

(SD 14)

When asked what it is that is so important about learning on the job and from experience, SD 14 replied that it was having the opportunity to learn from your mistakes and being able to identify the most effective way of doing things. SD 14 illustrated this by describing a case that he was involved in. SD 14 recounted how the SIO and he discussed the possible options in using the CCTV footage that had been obtained during a murder investigation:

We start talking about how can we prove that's our man in the shop? We've got nothing forensically to put him in the location it happened, so we've got to do our best to show that it is him in the CCTV. So for me, as a detective with previous experience, I go: "quite easy, we know where the camera is, we know where he's stood, we get someone the same height to stand there and then he'll be the same height at the wall as the other person and you'll know that person is the same height". But [names SIO] says, "Don't do it" so I asked why and he said, "it'll be more trouble than it's worth". So the books say "if you want to establish the height of someone, put someone in the same place so you know how tall they are", but it doesn't account for all the variables like are they running? Are they stood? Crouched? From previous experience [names SIO] said "don't bother it's a waste of time" but if we'd gone by the book, the tick list . . . so to me that's where a good SIO comes from.

(SD 14)

The skills required to conduct homicide investigations are extensive. Many of the interviewees struggled to answer the question of what skills are necessary for detectives today. Those often cited are related to being resilient and dogged, which are traits that cannot necessarily be trained or measured formally. Relatedly, they explained that it is difficult for SIOs today to be involved in the minutiae of homicide investigations, something that is largely due to the complex science and technology that features in many modern-day investigations. Consequently, they are reliant on other specialists in their team to feed the relevant information to them. This would also have repercussions for the way in which training is developed. Interestingly, the skills cited by the interviewees in this research coincide with the three clusters identified by Smith and Flanagan (2000, p. 24): management skills, investigative ability and knowledge levels. The long list of skills indicate that the role of the SIO, and indeed the detective, is an incredibly complex one, more so than it ever was in the past due to rapid developments in science and technology. Thus, it can be argued that it would be difficult for formal training alone to provide investigators with the skills that they need, highlighting again the importance of gaining experience "on the job".

It is important to acknowledge the backdrop against which this research was conducted, specifically the substantial budget cuts that the police have faced. Smith (2016, p. 179) notes that the coalition government's 2010 spending review "removed a significant amount of funding from police forces across the UK". Rogers (2014) notes that since 2010 police budgets have been reduced by 25%. It would seem that this has also affected training. Many detectives told of a lack of experienced SIOs and the inability of police services to release officers from Basic Command Units (BCUs) to the CID so that they can gain experience due to budget and staffing issues. This raises the question of how future detectives will benefit from what all interviewees considered to be the most effective way of learning. SD 8 expressed concern that there are not many SIOs working within their police service, which means that consequently there is a lack of mentors for new SIOs:

> Because there aren't many SIOs in the force and that's one thing I would say is lacking that mentor that you can shadow for some time until you feel confident really because every single murder investigation is different and each comes with different challenges, so I think that's the gap for me.
>
> (SD 8)

FD 2 explained that the major crime team that he used to be the head of was being reduced in size. He explained that this was a result of the number of murders that they were experiencing diminishing, and so the expenditure cannot be justified:

> A lot of it is driven by money. The problem is in my time when I was head of major crime, we were averaging anything between 15 and 20 murders a year, it has gone down now I think. I was only speaking to them last week and they're averaging less than 10 sometimes now, so to have a designated team on standby, you just can't afford it, so the team is being shrunk. So when I was head I had five DCIs and five DIs, I think they're now down to three DCIs and 3 DIs.
>
> (FD 2)

A similar point was made by FD 27, a former detective now working in a civilian post and based at a different police service to that of SD 8. He remarked that "there's more people wanting to be SIOs and less murders", indicating again that there will be fewer opportunities for less experienced officers to gain experience of murder investigations. Ultimately, if learning from others and gaining experience of homicide investigations are considered to be central to the training of detectives, the findings here give potential cause for concern for future detectives and approaches to training. Simply, if there are fewer opportunities for newer detectives to gain exposure to investigations, then this might impact upon their ability to lead investigations when they take the position of SIOs.

Conclusion

In this chapter we have considered the new challenges that appear to have emerged over the past four decades as a result of the changes that were described in Chapter one. It has been shown that recent developments have raised concern among many of the participants, in particular the lack of police investigative background of some of these team members. Although the interviewees stressed that investigations would not suffer significantly as a consequence of budget restrictions, its prevalence during the interviews is telling of the importance of it and of concerns around it. Lastly and crucially, we have seen that changes to legislation and guidance has led to homicide investigation becoming increasingly bureaucratic and detectives increasingly risk averse as a result. It would seem that an increase in bureaucracy has led to a feeling that they do too much that is not necessarily proportionate to the nature of the case being investigated. In the concluding chapter that follows, these issues, and others raised during this book, are summarised as we consider the broader implications.

Conclusion
The Past, Present and Future
of Homicide Investigation

The opening lines of this book described the long-awaited arrest of Peter Sutcliffe after an immense investigation by West Yorkshire Police, an investigation that was scrutinised during the eventual Byford enquiry and found to be flawed in many respects. This led to the investigation of homicide being placed firmly under the microscope for the first, but not the last, time. It was the intention of this book to document the key findings of doctoral research that explored the ways in which homicide investigations in England and Wales have changed since the 1980s and to reflect on the impact that these developments have had, both on investigations and on the homicide detective. This final chapter concludes the book by drawing together the past, present and future of homicide investigation in England and Wales. The changes that these investigations have been subject to since the 1980s are summarised and their impact on today's investigations outlined. In moving towards the future, that discussion is used to raise questions about what future research is needed to further explore some of the issues raised across the last three chapters.

Reviewing the Evidence

It cannot be denied that since the 1980s, the investigation of homicide in England and Wales has changed significantly. The extent of change has been such that almost every facet has been transformed, and there have been significant developments in respect of the scientific and technological tools that are available: the legislation, regulation and guidance governing investigations and investigators and the way in which investigations are run on a day-to-day basis, as well as changes to the culture and status of the homicide detective and detective work. Explaining why these changes have occurred is difficult because we have seen that the police are vulnerable to numerous influences at a societal and organisational level, which

DOI: 10.4324/9781003201298-5

have played some part in shaping homicide investigation in some way. Although my interest in examining changes from the 1980s was prompted by the view within the literature that the Yorkshire Ripper case and Byford enquiry marked the start of significant reform (Brain, 2010; Innes, 2003a), the picture is more complex, and attributing change to one case does not reveal the full story.

This research identified that changes to the investigation of homicide have been driven by a preoccupation with risk, the changing political landscape, reactions to miscarriages of justice and other cases and advances in science and technology. This, as we have seen, corresponds with what the literature reveals to drive changes in policing more broadly and in other organisations. However, it has also been acknowledged that the status of homicide is such that the public hold high expectations of the police in terms of how these crimes are investigated, which is also responsible for propelling change forward. It is therefore proffered that explaining change demands an integrated approach. Ultimately, the greatest challenge for the police service perhaps lies in achieving a balance between moving along with society, pacifying calls for action when something goes wrong to reassure the public and restore legitimacy, and maintaining perspective and proportionality when deciding what course of action to take.

Turning to the impact of change, a shortage of detectives has been identified, which has been reflected in other literature and recent media accounts. The implications for the future of homicide investigation are significant. Further research is needed, firstly, to fully understand why becoming a detective appears to be a less appealing prospect than in the past. Direct entry has been introduced partly in response to this shortage, but the widespread belief amongst detectives in this study was that a background in investigations in a policing capacity is important to being able to work on homicide investigations. Secondly, this research and the wider literature reveal continued concerns around the level of bureaucracy in homicide investigation and policing generally. The resultant risk aversion has also been recognised. Indeed, this is considered one explanation for the aforementioned shortage of detectives. It is suggested that a review of processes and procedures is necessary to identify whether there exists "burdensome bureaucracy". The detectives that I spoke to were not always specific about which processes and procedures were onerous, so a closer look at what exactly is considered to be problematic and unnecessary during the course of a homicide investigation is warranted. Other areas that we have looked at include concerns around police resources, and it is this that will be discussed in the following section.

Diminishing Resources and New Priorities

Significant cuts to public services, including the police, have taken place in recent years, and the detectives spoke of a move away from "throwing money at an investigation" to having to "do more with less". At the time that this research was conducted, concerns around resourcing of the police and *other* emergency services[1] were gaining traction. Moreover, there were growing concerns about acts of terrorism after several terrorist attacks occurred in London and Manchester across a short space of time in 2017. There were reports that the government was considering changing the police-funding formula, which would have affected larger forces, with more money going to smaller forces. This potential change was connected to the terrorist attacks and in response to warnings from the then Metropolitan Police commissioner that they could not endure further cuts (Toner, 2017). The possible ramifications for policing and the investigation of homicide were considered, and it was suggested that responses to growing concern about terrorist attacks might, in reality, prove detrimental to the funding of homicide investigations as terrorism moved higher up the agenda of the government, police and public. For the detectives that I spoke to, investigating homicide was seen as the "ultimate", and they felt that it holds a particular status amongst the public. However, as apprehension was growing about terrorism, it seemed possible that the status of other forms of homicide could shift.

In early 2022, however, as I write the conclusion to this book, the world is perhaps emerging from the coronavirus pandemic that has wreaked havoc on the world since March 2020. Now, with vaccinations seemingly paving the way for at least a "new normal" and providing us with further evidence of the impact of advances in science, attention is turning to the economic fallout. The impact that this will have on England and Wales, the wider world and, pertinently for our discussions, the investigation of homicide very much remains to be seen. However, when we consider that the detectives that I spoke to were concerned about the impact that tightening budgets were already having on homicide investigation, a somewhat concerning picture emerges about the impact that continued economic pressure might have. Conversely, the findings from my research did also reveal that the participants were of the view that a homicide investigation would not be impeded by budgetary concerns and that investigations would receive

1 In particular, concerns around the resourcing of the fire service were raised following the Grenfell fire disaster in London in June 2017.

the resourcing that they need. The picture here, therefore, remains somewhat unclear.

We have primarily considered the impact of change on the frontline – on investigative practice and the detective. It is necessary, however, to take a step back and consider the impact of change from a broader perspective. Whilst there is not the scope to fully explore this, it would be remiss to examine change and its impact, without speculating as to whether it has had any bearing upon the homicide detection rate or the likelihood of future investigative errors and miscarriages of justice.

The Obstinate Detection Rate

Although it can be argued that merely looking at the detection rate provides an inadequate measure of the efficiency and effectiveness of homicide investigations, it is an important consideration in light of the very high expectations that the public have of the police when they are investigating homicide (Stelfox, 2015). This is also one of the ways in which the police themselves measure performance in this area (Brookman and Innes, 2013). The numbers of homicides committed in England and Wales are amongst the lowest in the world (Brookman, Jones and Pike, 2017). In the year ending March 2021 there were 594 cases of homicide recorded in England and Wales (Office for National Statistics (ONS), 2022). A frequently used figure quoted by the participants regarding the numbers of homicides that are solved in England and Wales was "around 90%". A review of the literature supports this. Brookman, Maguire and Maguire (2018) found that the homicide detection rate has been around 90% since the 2000s. However, the detection rate has declined from an average of 94% during the 1960s (Brookman, Maguire and Maguire, 2018)[2]. A detection rate of "around 90%" is high, which is possibly why it has not been subject to much discussion. In addition, the majority of homicides are classed as "self-solvers" (Innes, 2003a), where the perpetrator is quickly identified (see Brodeur and Dupont, 2006 for similar results in Quebec), which might also explain the lack of critical attention to the detection rate.

However, the question that arises is, why, despite all the developments that have occurred, which have aimed to improve effectiveness and that have, according to the data, generally been positive in their impact, have we not seen an improvement in the detection rate? The findings of my research

---

2 Interestingly, the homicide rate in the USA has declined significantly and is around 65% (Brookman, Maguire and Maguire, 2018).

might provide some explanation. It has been established that risk aversion is such that some detectives feel unsure of using intuition or creativity, which presents the possibility that difficult cases, which might require such an approach to move them forward, might be compromised. It has also been found that advances in science and technology have led to the weakening of what are considered traditional detective skills, and science and technology sometimes relied upon to the exclusion of other avenues. It was also said that consequently, when cases do not feature some aspect of scientific or technological evidence, it can be difficult to progress them. It is possible that this might help us to explain the detection rate, particularly since several cases in which these problems were present were cited in this research and which remain unsolved. These issues are arguably compounded by the concerns that were raised around detective training. Although it was agreed that training had improved in many respects, it was believed that exposure to investigations remains the most important part of detective training. However, it was also reported that budget cuts have meant that opportunities to release officers from BCUs to experience major crime investigations have been reduced. Moreover, there has been little evaluation of the PIP (James and Mills, 2012; Tong, 2009), and so the findings of this research are further indication that this should be addressed, for the identified shortcomings in training are potentially influencing the detection rate. Additionally, a shortage of detectives has been identified by both existing literature and the current research, and it is possible that this is having a detrimental impact upon whether or not investigations are progressed.

It is difficult to definitively say why the detection rate has remained rather static, and there are undoubtedly other factors that will affect it, but it is reasonable to surmise that the challenges that have been discussed in this book, and others detailed in the thesis itself, are playing at least some part in encumbering the detection rate. Ultimately, although the detection rate is certainly high, it would seem that there is no room for complacency and that a further increase in the detection rate might be possible if the concerns that have been raised here are tackled.

Have Lessons Been Learned?

If, as the detectives and the literature suggest, investigative errors or miscarriages of justice are often an important motive for change, it is necessary to consider the extent to which the many reforms that have taken place across the past few decades have reduced the likelihood of these problems arising again. The general view of the participants was that we are unlikely to see the level of occurrence of miscarriages of justice that we witnessed in the past because of the changes that have been made. For example, the changes that have taken place have increased accountability, which will have reduced the chances of such occurrences. However, there is also evidence to the contrary.

At the end of 2016 the IPCC, now known as the IOPC, began an investigation into the Metropolitan Police's handling of the murders of four men – Anthony Walgate, Gabriel Kovari, Daniel Whitworth and Jack Taylor – in London between 2014 and 2015. Stephen Port administered the so-called "date rape" drug, gamma-hydroxybutyrate (GBH) (*BBC*, 2021c), to the men before killing them. Although Port was ultimately convicted and received a whole life term for the murders, concerns were raised about police failures to identify the deaths as homicides and link them. It has been suggested that institutional homophobia (Davies, 2021) was a factor in the shortcomings of this investigation, raising questions about how far mindsets have changed and whether they have changed to the extent suggested by the findings of my research, which were discussed in Chapter two. The investigation by the IPCC was concluded in 2018, in the wake of anger from the families at the delays and reports of officers refusing to answer questions during the investigation (De Simone, 2018). It found that the officers in question "did not have a case to answer for misconduct or gross misconduct. We also agreed that the performance of nine officers fell below the standard required and they will need to undergo measures to ensure performance is improved" (IOPC, 2020, para 4)[3]. However, the inquest into the deaths of the men ruled in 2021 that the failings of the Metropolitan Police *had* likely led to more deaths (Davies, 2021). This led the IOPC to announce in late 2021 that they were considering whether a reinvestigation is necessary. At the time of writing, a decision on this has yet to be announced.

Responsible for investigating alleged cases of miscarriages of justice and often dealing with serious crimes including homicide, the Criminal Cases Review Commission (CCRC) was established in 1997 and, in that time, has referred 762 cases to the Court of Appeal (CCRC, 2021). The CCRC Annual Report for 2015/16 stated that over the year they had seen a "steady stream of miscarriages of justice" (CCRC, 2016, p. 11) and that over the last three years they had seen an increase of approximately 50% in the number of applications that they received. Twenty-two percent of these referrals were for homicide convictions. Although in this report the CCRC did not provide much detail about the cases that they had dealt with, what it did reveal was that the cases that have been referred to the appeal courts are relatively recent; for example, two homicide cases were from

---

3 Further details are not yet available as the IOPC (2021) report into this case will not be published until all proceedings have concluded.

2000 and 2006. That these cases were subject to modern-day investigative processes further suggests that they are by no means infallible. In 2020/21 the CCRC received 1,142 applications, 14% fewer than the previous year, raising questions about the impact of the global pandemic upon such cases (CCRC, 2021). Although it is important to note that this body has itself not been immune from criticism and it has been accused of not being fit for purpose and of "failing to fulfil its original promise" (Poyser, Nurse and Milne, 2018, p. 89), the work that it does serves to perhaps provide us with further evidence that the policing of homicide and other crimes remains in need of close attention. Additionally, as was outlined in the introduction, a review of 40 years of public enquiries into murder investigations found that the same problems arise repeatedly, including issues around leadership, the skills of the SIO and information management (Roycroft, 2008). This too raises questions as to how far the police, despite changes being made, learn from such cases and, pertinently, about the efficacy of the changes that have been made over the last four decades.

An End Note

The central aim of the research upon which this book is based was to explore change, and the detectives sometimes demonstrated differing views on the subject. I end this book in the same way that I ended the thesis, by revisiting the one question on which there was resounding agreement amongst the participants. That question was "What was/is the most rewarding part of being a detective working on homicide investigations?"

It's dealing with families of murder victims, it is such a privilege.

(FD 9)

I do draw an awful lot of satisfaction from engaging with families . . . what I can do is bring the case to a conclusion where they are happy that that's the right conclusion and justice has been done.

(SD 13)

Throughout this book many questions have been raised about the ways in which homicides in England and Wales are investigated, and it has become clear that, although many new opportunities have arisen over the years, many new challenges are being faced. However, what also emerged was that, for the detectives that I interviewed, helping the families who have lost a loved one to homicide and bringing the offender to justice remains the most rewarding part of investigating homicide, showing that for them some things have not changed.

References

Al Mutawa, N., Baggili, I. and Marrington, A. (2012) 'Forensic analysis of social networking applications on mobile devices', *Digital Investigation*, 9, pp. 524–533.

Allsop, C. (2018) *Cold case reviews. DNA, detective work and unsolved major crimes*. Oxford: Oxford University Press.

Allsop, C. and Pike, S. (2019) 'Investigating homicide: Back to the future', *Journal of Criminological Research, Policy and Practice*, 5(3), pp. 229–239.

Amankwaa, A.O. and McCartney, C. (2021) 'The effectiveness of the current use of forensic DNA in criminal investigation in England and Wales', *WIREs Forensic Science*, pp. 1–19.

Association of Chief Police Officers (2006) *Murder investigation manual*. 3rd edn. Wyboston: National Centre for Policing Excellence.

Atkin, H. and Roach, J. (2015) 'Spot the difference: Comparing current and historic homicide investigations in the UK', *Journal of Cold Case Review*, 1(1), pp. 5–21.

Baranowski, A.M., et al. (2018) 'The CSI-education effect: Do potential criminals benefit from forensic TV series?' *International Journal of Law, Crime and Justice*, 52, pp. 86–97.

Bayerl, P.S., et al. (2013) 'The role of macro context for the link between technological and organisational change', *Journal of Organisational Change Management*, 26(5), pp. 793–810.

BBC (2021a) 'Bibaa Henry and Nicole Smallman: Met PCs jailed for crime scene images', *BBC*, 6 December. Available at: Bibaa Henry and Nicole Smallman: Met PCs jailed for crime scene images – BBC News (Accessed: 22 January 2022).

BBC (2021b) 'Colin Pitchfork recalled to jail after approaching young women', *BBC*, 22 November. Available at: Colin Pitchfork recalled to jail after approaching young women – BBC News (Accessed: 20 January 2022).

BBC (2021c) 'Stephen Port: MET Police failings led to more deaths', *BBC*, 10 December. Available at: Stephen Port: Met Police failings led to more deaths – BBC News (Accessed: 10 January 2022).

Beauragard, E. and Martineau, M. (2014) 'No body, no crime? The role of forensic awareness in avoiding police detection in cases of sexual homicide', *Journal of Criminal Justice*, 42, pp. 213–220.

Beckley, R. and Birkinshaw, J. (2009) 'Dealing with a crisis – What the police have learnt and what others can learn from the police', *Policing*, 3(1), pp. 7–11.

Bowling, B., Reiner, R. and Sheptycki, J. (2019) *The politics of the police*. 5th edn. Oxford: Oxford University Press.

Brain, T. (2010) *A history of policing in England and Wales from 1974. A turbulent journey*. Oxford: Oxford University Press.

Bramley, B. (2009) 'DNA databases', in Fraser, J. and Williams, R. (eds.) *Handbook of forensic science*. London: Willan Publishing, pp. 309–336.

Brodeur, J-P. (2009) *The policing web*. Oxford: Oxford University Press.

Brodeur, J-P. and Dupont, B. (2006) 'Knowledge workers or "knowledge" workers?' *Policing and Society*, 16(1), pp. 7–26.

Brookman, F. (2015) 'Researching homicide offenders, offences and detectives using qualitative methods', in Copes, H. and Miller, M. (eds.) *The handbook of qualitative criminology*. Oxon: Routledge, pp. 236–252.

Brookman, F. and Innes, M. (2013) 'The problem of success: What is a "good" homicide investigation?', *Policing and Society: An International Journal of Research and Policy*, pp. 1–19.

Brookman, F. and Jones, H. (2021) 'Capturing killers: The construction of CCTV evidence during homicide investigations', *Policing and Society: An International Journal of Research and Policy*. doi: 10.1080/10439463.2021.1879075.

Brookman, F., Jones, H. and Pike, S. (2017) 'Homicide in Britain', in Brookman, F., Maguire, E. R. and Maguire, M. (eds.) *Handbook of homicide*. Chichester: Wiley-Blackwell, pp. 320–344.

Brookman, F. and Lloyd-Evans, M. (2015) 'A decade of homicide debriefs: What has been learnt?' *The Journal of Homicide and Major Crime Investigation*, 10(1), pp. 14–45.

Brookman, F., Maguire, E.R. and Maguire, M. (2017) 'Introduction: Homicide in global perspective', in Brookman, F., Maguire, E.R. and Maguire, M. (eds.) *Handbook of homicide*. Chichester: Wiley-Blackwell, pp. 19–24.

Brookman, F., Maguire, E.R. and Maguire, M. (2018) 'What factors influence whether homicide cases are solved? Insights from qualitative research with detectives in Great Britain and the United States', *Homicide Studies*, 23(2), pp. 145–174.

Brookman, F., Pike, S. and Maguire, E.R. (2019) 'Dancing around *Miranda*: The effects of legal reform on homicide detectives in the USA and the UK', *Criminal Law Bulletin*, 55(5), pp. 725–763.

Brookman, F. and Wakefield, A. (2009) 'Criminal investigation', in Wakefield, A. and Fleming, J. (eds.) *The Sage dictionary of policing*. London: Sage Publications, pp. 65–70.

Brown, K.M. and Keppel, R.D. (2012) 'Child abduction murder: The impact of forensic evidence on solvability', *The Journal of Forensic Science*, 57(2), pp. 353–363.

Bryett, K. (1999) 'The policing dynamic', *Policing: An International Journal of Police Strategies & Management*, 22(1), pp. 30–44.

Byford, L. (1981) *The Yorkshire Ripper case: Review of the police investigation of the case*. London: Home Office.

Cape, E. and Young, R. (eds.) (2008) *Regulating policing. The police and criminal evidence act 1984: Past, present and future.* Oxford: Hart Publishing.

Carson, D. (1996) 'Risking legal repercussions', in Kemshall, H. and Pritchard, J. (eds.) *Good practice in risk assessment and risk management.* London: Jessica Kingsley Publishers, pp. 3–12.

Carson, D. (2007) 'Models of investigation', in Newburn, T., Williamson, T. and Wright, A. (eds.) *Handbook of criminal investigation.* London: Willan Publishing, pp. 407–425.

Christie, N. (1986) 'The ideal victim', in Fattah, E. (ed.) *From crime policy to victim policy.* Basingstoke: Macmillan, pp. 17–30.

Cole, S. and Dioso-Villa, R. (2009) 'Investigating the 'CSI effect' effect: Media and litigation crisis in criminal law', *Stanford Law Review*, 61(6), pp. 1335–1374.

Compston, H. and Lowbridge, C. (2018) 'How familial DNA trapped a murderer for the first time', *BBC*, 22 November. Available at: How familial DNA trapped a murderer for the first time – BBC News (Accessed: 21 January 2022).

Cook, T. and Tattersall, A. (2010) *Blackstone's senior investigating officers' handbook.* 2nd edn. Oxford: Oxford University Press.

Cooney, M. (2017) 'Social and legal responses to homicide', in Brookman, F. Maguire, E.R. and Maguire, M. (eds.) *The handbook on homicide.* Chichester: Wiley-Blackwell, pp. 54–70.

Cooper, A. and Mason, L. (2009) 'Forensic resources and criminal investigations', in Fraser, J. and Williams, R. (eds.) *Handbook of forensic science.* London: Willan Publishing, pp. 285–308.

Crawford, R., Disney, R. and Innes, D. (2015) 'Funding the English & Welsh police services: From boom to bust?' *Institute for Fiscal Studies*, 17 November. Available at: https://ifs.org.uk/publications/8049 (Accessed: 10 March 2022).

Criminal Cases Review Commission (2016) *Annual report and accounts 2015/2016.* Available at: HC244 – CCRC Criminal Cases Review Commission Annual Report and Accounts 2015/2016 (Accessed: 11 February 2022).

Criminal Cases Review Commission (2021) *Annual report and accounts 2020/2021.* Available at: CCRC-Annual-Report-and-Accounts-2020–2021.pdf (Accessed: 11 February 2022).

Davies, C. (2021) 'Met failings probably a factor in deaths of Stephen Port victims, says inquest', *The Guardian*, 10 December. Available at: Met failings probably a factor in deaths of Stephen Port victims, says inquest | Police | The Guardian (Accessed: 10 January 2022).

De Simone, D. (2018) 'Stephen Port: Officers refuse to answer watchdog's questions', *BBC*, 26 July. Available at: Stephen Port: Officers refuse to answer watchdog's questions – BBC News (Accessed: 12 March 2022).

Disney, R. and Simpson, P. (2017) 'Police workforce and funding in England and Wales', *Institute for Fiscal Studies*. Available at: https://ifs.org.uk/uploads/publications/bns/bn208.pdf (Accessed: 19 August 2022).

Downes, D. and Morgan, R. (2007) 'No turning back: The politics of law and order into the millennium', in Maguire, M., Morgan, R. and Reiner, R. (eds.) *The Oxford handbook of criminology*, 4th edn. Oxford: Oxford University Press, pp. 201–240.

Downes, D. and Morgan, R. (2012) 'Overtaking on the left? The politics of law and order in the "big society"', in Maguire, M., Morgan, R. and Reiner, R. (eds.) *The Oxford handbook of criminology*. 5th edn. Oxford: Oxford University Press, pp. 182–205.

Durnal, E. W. (2010) 'Crime Scene Investigation (as seen on TV)', *Forensic Science International*, 199, pp. 1–5.

Emsley, C. (2008) 'The birth and development of the police', in Newburn, T. (ed.) *Handbook of policing*. 2nd edn. Cullompton: Willan Publishing, pp. 72–89.

Flanagan, R. (2008) *The review of policing. Final report*. Available at: flanagan-review-of-policing-20080201.pdf (justiceinspectorates.gov.uk) (Accessed: 11 March 2022).

Fleming, J. (2009) 'Civilianisation', in Wakefield, A. and Fleming, J. (eds.) *The Sage dictionary of policing*. London: Sage Publications, pp. 25–28.

Fox, J. (2014) 'Is there room for flair in a police major crime investigation?' *The Journal of Homicide and Major Crime Investigation*, 19(1), pp. 2–19.

Fraser, J. and Williams, R. (2009) 'Glossary', in Fraser, J. and Williams, R. (eds.) *Handbook of forensic science*. London: Willan Publishing, pp. 623–642.

Gerrard, G. (2007) 'CCTV and major incident investigation: Professionalising the police approach', *Journal of Homicide and Major Incident Investigation*, 3(2), pp. 7–20.

Gibbs, F. (1985) 'Biggest change for 50 years; Police and criminal evidence act 1984 co come into force', *The Times*, 31 December. Available at: https://go-gale-com.bathspa.idm.oclc.org/ps/i.do?p=STND&u=bsuc&id=GALE%7CA1179358 72&v=2.1&it=r&sid=ebsco (Accessed: 13 May 2021).

Glynn, J.J. and Murphy, M.P. (1996) 'Public management: Failing accountabilities and failing performance review', *International Journal of Public Sector Management*, 9(5/6), pp. 125–137.

Golding, B. and Savage, S.P. (2008) 'Leadership and performance management', in Newburn, T. (ed.) *Handbook of policing*. 2nd edn. Cullompton: Willan Publishing., pp. 725–759.

GOV.UK (2011) *The future of the national policing improvement agency*. Available at: The future of the National Policing Improvement Agency – GOV.UK (www.gov.uk) (Accessed: 25 January 2022).

GOV.UK (2020) *Policing gets biggest funding boost in decade to put more bobbies on the beat*. Available at: Policing gets biggest funding boost in decade to put more bobbies on the beat – GOV.UK (www.gov.uk) (Accessed: 26 January 2022).

Green, T. and Gates, A. (2014) 'Understanding the process of professionalisation in the police organisation', *The Police Journal: Theory, Practice and Principles*, 87(2), pp. 75–91.

Hannibal, M. and Mountford, L. (2002) *The law of civil and criminal evidence: Principles and practice*. Harlow: Longman.

Heaton, R. (2011) 'We could be criticised! Policing and risk aversion', *Policing*, 5(1), pp. 75–86.

Her Majesty's Inspectorate of Constabulary (2004) *Modernising the police service: A thematic inspection of workforce modernisation – The role, management and deployment of police staff in the police service of England and Wales*. London: Her Majesty's Inspectorate of Constabulary.

Her Majesty's Inspectorate of Constabulary (2014) *Policing in austerity: Meeting the challenge*. London: Her Majesty's Inspectorate of Constabulary.

Her Majesty's Inspectorate of Constabulary (2017) *PEEL: Police effectiveness 2016. A national overview*. London: Her Majesty's Inspectorate of Constabulary.

Her Majesty's Inspectorate of Constabulary (2018) *PEEL: Police effectiveness 2017. A national overview*. London: Her Majesty's Inspectorate of Constabulary.

Heslop, R. (2011) 'The British police service: Professionalisation or "McDonaldisation"?' *International Journal of Police Science and Management*, 13(4), pp. 275–285.

Hobbs, D. (1988) *Doing the business*. Oxford: Oxford University Press.

Hood, C., Rothstein, H. and Baldwin, R. (2001) *The government of risk: Understanding risk regulation regimes*. Oxford: Oxford University Press.

Huey, L. (2010) 'I've seen this on CSI: Criminal investigators' perceptions about the management of public expectations in the field', *Crime, Media, Culture*, 6(1), pp. 49–68.

Hutter, B. and Lloyd-Bostock, S (1990) 'The power of accidents: The social and psychological impact of accidents and the enforcement of safety regulations', *The British Journal of Criminology*, 30(4), pp. 409–422.

Independent Office for Police Conduct (2020) *Stephen Port murders – Metropolitan police service*. Available at: Stephen Port murders – Metropolitan Police Service | Independent Office for Police Conduct (Accessed: 10 February 2022).

Independent Office for Police Conduct (2021) *IOPC considering reopening investigation into Met Police handling of deaths of Anthony Walgate, Gabriel Kovari, Daniel Whitworth and Jack Taylor*. Available at: IOPC considering reopening investigation into Met Police handling of deaths of Anthony Walgate, Gabriel Kovari, Daniel Whitworth and Jack Taylor | Independent Office for Police Conduct (Accessed: 10 February 2022).

Independent Office for Police Conduct (2022) *Thematic learning issued to address cultural concerns in nine linked investigations – Metropolitan police service, June 2018*. Available at: Thematic learning issued to address cultural concerns in nine linked investigations – Metropolitan Police Service, June 2018 | Independent Office for Police Conduct (Accessed: 28 January 2022).

Innes, M. (2001) 'Control creep', *Sociological Research Online*, 6(3). Available at: www.socresonline.org.uk/6/3/innes.html (Accessed: 18 January 2022).

Innes, M. (2002) 'The "process structures" of police homicide investigation', *The British Journal of Criminology*, 42(4), pp. 669–688.

Innes, M. (2003a) *Investigating murder. Detective work and the police response to criminal homicide*. London: Oxford University Press.

Innes, M. (2003b) 'Signal crimes: Detective work, mass media and constructing collective memory', in P. Mason (ed.) *Criminal visions: Representations of crime and justice*. Cullompton: Willan Publishing, pp. 51–73.

Innes, M. (2010) 'The art, craft and science of policing', in Cane, P. and Kritzer, H. (eds.) *The Oxford handbook of empirical legal research*. Oxford: Oxford University Press, pp. 9–36.

James, A. (2013) *Examining intelligence-led policing. Developments in research, policy and practice*. Hampshire: Palgrave Macmillan.

James, A. and Mills, M. (2012) 'Does ACPO know best: To what extent may the PIP programme provide a template for the professionalisation of policing?' *The Police Journal*, 85, pp. 133–149.

Jewkes, Y. (2011) *Media and crime*. 2nd edn. London: Sage.

Jones, D., Grieve, J. and Milne, B. (2008) 'The case to review murder investigations', *Policing*, 2(4), pp. 470–480.

Kemshall, H. (2003) *Understanding risk in criminal justice*. Maidenhead: Open University Press.

Kemshall, H. (2009) 'Working with sex offenders in a climate of public blame and anxiety: How to make defensible decisions for risk', *Journal of Sexual Aggression*, 15(3), pp. 331–343.

Laming, H. (2003) *The Victoria Climbie inquiry: Report of an inquiry by Lord Laming*. London: The Stationery Office.

Laming, H. (2009) *The protection of children in England: A progress report*. London: House of Commons.

Littlechild, B. (2008) 'Child protection social work: Risks of fears and fears of risks – Impossible tasks from impossible goals?' *Social Policy and Administration*, 42(6), pp. 662–675.

Macpherson, W. (1999) *Report of an inquiry into the investigation of the murder of Stephen Lawrence*. London: Her Majesty's Stationery Office.

Maguire, M. (1988) 'Effects of the "P.A.C.E." provisions on detention and questioning: Some preliminary findings', *The British Journal of Criminology*, 28(1), pp. 19–43.

Maguire, M. (2008) 'Criminal investigation and crime control', in Newburn, T. (ed.) *Handbook of policing*. 2nd edn. Cullompton: Willan Publishing, pp. 430–465.

Maguire, M. and Norris, C. (1992) *The conduct and supervision of criminal investigation*. Royal Commission on Criminal Justice Research Study No. 5. London: Her Majesty's Stationery Office.

Manning, P.K. (1977) *Police work: The social organisation of policing*. Cambridge: MIT Press.

Marx, G. (1988) *Undercover police surveillance in America*. Berkeley: University of California Press.

Matassa, M. and Newburn, T. (2007) 'Social context of criminal investigation', in Newburn, T., Williamson, T. and Wright, A. (eds.) *Handbook of criminal investigation*. Cullompton: Willan Publishing, pp. 41–67.

Mawby, R. C. (2012) *Policing images: Policing, communication and legitimacy*. London: Routledge.

McCartney, C. and Shorter, L. (2019) 'Exacerbating injustice: Post-conviction disclosure in England and Wales', *International Journal of Law, Crime and Justice*, 59. doi: 10.1016/j.ijlcj.2019.03.007.

Milivojevic, S. and McGovern, A. (2014) 'The death of Jill Meagher: Crime and punishment on social media', *International Journal for Crime, Justice and Social Democracy*, 3(3), pp. 22–39.

Mooney, J. (2010) 'HOLMES: From inception to modern day via lessons learned', *The Journal of Homicide and Major Incident Investigation*, 6(1), pp. 31–50.

Morris, B. (2007) 'History of criminal investigation', in Newburn, T., Williamson, T. and Wright, A. (eds.) *Handbook of criminal investigation*. Cullompton: Willan Publishing, pp. 15–40.

Munro, E. (2010) 'Learning to reduce risk in child protection', *British Journal of Social Work*, 40, pp. 1135–1151.

National Police Chiefs' Council (2021) *Major crime investigation manual (MCIM 2021)*. Available at: Major-Crime-Investigation-Manual-Nov-2021.pdf (college. police.uk) (Accessed: 18 January 2022).

National Policing Improvement Agency (2011) *Practice advice on the use of CCTV in criminal investigations*. London: National Policing Improvement Agency.

Nicol, C., Innes, M., Gee, D. and Feist, A. (2004) *Reviewing murder investigations: An analysis of progress reviews from six police forces*. London: Home Office.

O'Neill, M. (2018) *Key challenges in criminal investigation*. Bristol: Policy Press.

Ofcom (2020) *Adults' media use and attitudes: Report 2020*. Available at: www. ofcom.org.uk/__data/assets/pdf_file/0031/196375/adults-media-use-and-attitudes-2020-report.pdf (Accessed: 11 February 2022).

Office for National Statistics (2022) *Homicide in England and Wales: Year ending March 2021*. Available at: Homicide in England and Wales – Office for National Statistics (ons.gov.uk) (Accessed: 18 January 2022).

Pike, S. (2018) *A critical exploration of changes to the investigation of homicide in England and Wales from the 1980s to the present day*. PhD Thesis. University of South Wales. Available at: Sophie_Pike_PhD_FINAL_PDF.pdf (southwales. ac.uk) (Accessed: 25 March 2022).

Pike, S., Allsop, C. and Brookman, F. (2020) 'Homicide in context', in Loucks, N., Smith Holt, S. and Adler, J.R. (eds.) *Why we kill: Understanding violence across cultures and disciplines*. 2nd edn. London: Routledge, pp. 19–33.

Police Federation (2021) *Police funding: The facts are clear – The police service, our members are held in contempt by the government*. Available at: Police funding: "The facts are clear – the Police service, our members, are held in contempt by the Government" (polfed.org) (Accessed: 26 January 2022).

Police Federation (no date) *Detectives in crisis*. Available at: Detectives in Crisis (polfed.org) (Accessed: 28 January 2022).

Poyser, S. and Milne, B. (2011) 'Miscarriages of justice: A call for continued research focusing on reforming the investigative process', *The British Journal of Forensic Practice*, 13(2), pp. 61–71.

Poyser, S., Nurse, A. and Milne, B. (2018) *Miscarriages of justice: Causes, consequences, and remedies*. Bristol: Policy Press.

Reiner, R. (1992) 'Policing a postmodern society', *The Modern Law Review*, 55(6), pp. 761–781.

Reiner, R. (2007) 'Media-made criminality: The representation of crime in the media', in Maguire, M., Morgan, R. and Reiner, R. (eds.) *The Oxford handbook of criminology*. 4th edn. Oxford: Oxford University Press, pp. 302–337.

Reiner, R. (2010) *The politics of the police*. 4th edn. Oxford: Oxford University Press.

Reppetto, T.A. (1978) 'The state of the art, science and craft?' *Police Studies: The International Review of Police Development*, 1(3), pp. 5–10.

Ritzer, G. (2004) *The McDonaldization of society*. Revised new century edition. London: Sage Publications.

Ritzer, G. (2015) *The McDonaldization of society*. 8th edn. London: Sage Publications.

Robbins, S.P. and Judge, T.A. (2008) *Essentials of organisational behaviour*. 13th edn. Essex: Pearson Limited.

Rogers, C. (2014) 'Police accountability in the age of austerity', *Police Journal: Theory, Practice and Principles*, 87, pp. 1–2.

Rogers, C. and Gravelle, J. (2012) 'UK policing and change: Reflections for policing worldwide', *Review of European Studies*, 4(1), pp. 42–52.

Rossmo, D.K. (2008) *Criminal investigative failures*. Boca Raton: CRC Press.

Rossmo, D.K. (2016) 'Case rethinking: A protocol for reviewing criminal investigations', *Police, Practice and Research. An International Journal*, 17(3), pp. 212–228.

Roux, C. and Robertson, J. (2009) 'The development and enhancement of forensic expertise: Higher education and in-service training', in Fraser, J. and Williams, R. (eds.) *Handbook of forensic science*. London: Willan Publishing, pp. 572–601.

Roycroft, M. (2008) 'Historical analysis of public inquiries of homicide investigations', *The Journal of Homicide and Major Incident Investigation*, 4(2), pp. 43–58.

Rubin, G.R. (2011) 'Calling in the Met: Serious crime investigation involving Scotland Yard and provincial police forces in England and Wales, 1906–1939', *Legal Studies*, 31(3), pp. 411–411.

Sanders, C.B. and Hannem, S. (2012) 'Policing "the risky": Technology and surveillance in everyday patrol work', *Canadian Review of Sociology*, 49(4), pp. 389–411.

Savage, S.P. (2007) 'Give and take: The bifurcation of police reform in Britain', *The Australian and New Zealand Journal of Criminology*, 40(3), pp. 313–334.

Savage, S.P. (2008) *Police reform: Forces for change*. Oxford: Oxford University Press.

Savage, S.P., Grieve, J. and Poyser, S. (2007) 'Putting wrongs to right: Campaigns against miscarriages of justice', *Criminology and Criminal Justice*, 7(1), pp. 83–105.

Savage, S.P. and Milne, B. (2007) 'Miscarriages of justice', in Newburn, T., Williamson, T. and Wright, A. (eds.) *Handbook of criminal investigation*. Cullompton: Willan Publishing, pp. 610–627.

Sendrea, M. (2017) 'Drivers of organisational changes', *Business and Administration*, 2(100), pp. 16–23.

Senior, P., Crowther-Dowey, C. and Long, M. (2007) *Understanding modernisation in criminal justice*. Berkshire: Open University Press.

Shpayer-Makov, H. (2004) 'Becoming a police detective in Victorian and Edwardian London', *Policing and Society: An International Journal of Research and Policy*, 14(3), pp. 250–268.

Smith, N. and Flanagan, C. (2000) *The effective detective: Identifying the skills of an effective SIO*. London: Home Office.

Smith, R. (2016) 'Policing in austerity: Time to go lean?' *International Journal of Emergency Services*, 5(2), pp. 174–183.

Stelfox, P. (2009) *Criminal investigation. An introduction to principles and practice*. Devon: Willan Publishing.

Stelfox, P. (2015) 'The evolution of homicide investigation in the UK', *The Journal of Homicide and Major Incident Investigation*, 10(2), pp. 92–106.

Surveillance Camera Commissioner (2017) *A national surveillance camera strategy for England and Wales*. Available at: A National Surveillance Camera Strategy for England and Wales (publishing.service.gov.uk) (Accessed: 31 January 2022).

Taupin, J. (2013) *Introduction to forensic DNA evidence for criminal justice professionals*. Boca Raton: CRC Press.

Toner, J. (2017) 'Government considering U-turn on funding formula', *Police Oracle*, 21 June. Available at: www.policeoracle.com/news/Government-considering-U-turn-on-funding-formula_95078.html (Accessed: 11 March 2022).

Tong, S. (2009) 'Professionalising investigations', in Tong, S., Bryant, R. and Horvath, M. (eds.) *Understanding criminal investigation*. Chichester: Wiley-Blackwell, pp. 197–216.

Tong, S. and Bowling, B. (2006) 'Art, craft and science of detective work', *The Police Journal*, 79, pp. 323–329.

Turnell, A., Munro, E. and Murphy, T. (2013) 'Soft is hardest: Leading for learning in child protection services following a child fatality', *Child Welfare*, 92(2), pp. 199–217.

Van Dijk, A., Hoogewoning, F. and Punch, M. (2015) *What matters in policing? Change, values and leadership in turbulent times*. Bristol: Policy Press.

Walsh, D. and Bull, R. (2010) 'What really is effective in interviews with suspects? A study comparing interviewing skills against interviewing outcomes', *Legal and Criminological Psychology*, 15, pp. 305–321.

Weick, K.E. and Quinn, R.E. (1999) 'Organisational change and development', *Annual Review of Psychology*, 50, pp. 361–386.

Westera, N.J., et al. (2016) 'The prospective detective: Developing the effective detective of the future', *Policing and Society: An International Journal of Research and Policy*, 26(2), pp. 197–209.

White, R.M. and Greenwood, J.J.D. (1988) 'DNA fingerprinting and the law', *Modern Law Review*, 51(2), pp. 145–155.

Williams, R. and Johnson, P. (2007) 'Trace biometrics and criminal investigation', in Newburn, T., Williamson, T. and Wright, A. (eds.) *Handbook of criminal investigation*. Cullompton: Willan Publishing, pp. 357–380.

Williams, R. and Weetman, J. (2013) 'Enacting forensics in homicide investigations', *Policing and Society*, 23(3), pp. 376–389.

Index

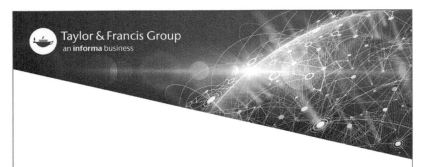